A LEGACY

OF LOVE

VOLUME I

A LEGACY OF LOVE

VOLUME ONE

The Return to Mount Shasta and Beyond

With

Saint Germain

As Channeled Through

Philip Burley

Mastery Press

Phoenix, Arizona

Cover and Book Designer
Jennifer Fleischmann
Layout Artist
Lynn Mathers

Photograph of Philip Burley
Final Focus
Wilmington, Delaware

Published by
AIM Publishers, now known as

A Publishing Division of
Adventures in Mastery (AIM), LLC

Mastery Press
P.O. Box 43548, Phoenix, AZ 85080

ISBN 978-1-883389-56-7
eISBN: 978-1-883389-24-6

Fourth Printing
Printed in the United States of America

I dedicate this book with eternal gratitude to all my spirit guides and teachers both in the spirit world and on earth, including beloved Saint Germain who told me in the beginning, "All of your guides and teachers are as important to you as I am." He stressed, in his usual humble and sincere way, that he is a part of a body of helpers and that all are needed. None of this book would be possible without all of them. You have all served me and this mission of being a bridge between two worlds over and above the call of duty. I am forever in your debt as are all of those who have benefitted in small and large ways in your ever-loving, ever-giving service.

Philip Burley
April 28, 2003

Acknowledgments

 IRST, I WOULD LIKE TO RECOGNIZE A CIRCLE OF FRIENDS who pray for this work. Their prayers are hidden but contribute greatly to what I do in keeping everything on course.

My dear wife, Vivien, is always beside me, giving her invaluable support in innumerable ways, without which I would have had a hard time coming this far in my private as well as public life. She, more than anyone, experiences daily the full reality of living with someone whose gift is so very unusual and who is always in demand. Vivien, the world may not know it but *I* know it, you are a saint! My gratitude, for your presence in my life for 34 years, knows no bounds.

My heart is so deeply moved by the great encouragement in prayers, letters, and conversations that I have received from Sara O'Meara, who believes in me so fully. She has been a true friend in all that I have undertaken in these past seven years in the Valley of the Sun, Phoenix, Arizona. Her life experience and the wisdom she has gained and shares, has served as a great example to me and has spurred me on and on! From Sara, among other things, I have especially learned about faith and courage. She lives what Jesus taught. I and countless others are recipients of her constant caring and goodwill.

Lynn Mathers, how could I have come this far without you? You are an executive's dream of the ideal administrative assistant. Your steadfastness over the years in helping with my outreach to the public is met with eternal gratitude. As you well know, I take every opportunity I can to say, "thank you." Thank you, dear friend.

Then there are the anonymous donors to our non-profit organization *Association for Internal Mastery* also known as *AIM*, to whom I owe a great debt of gratitude. "Ideals" are just that until someone can marry ideals with a concrete plan and the financial funds to make the ideals a reality. You know who you are and you know how grateful I am and how much I am in your spiritual debt. You have made the forward movement of my work possible. A thousand, thousand thanks!

The credit for the manuscript of *A Legacy of Love* and final preparations to turn it into a published book go to Lynn Mathers, Nancy Barton, and Sally Cole who worked long hours to transcribe many years' worth of my channeling Saint Germain. That the three of you, with already busy schedules, took it upon yourselves to help the cause of Saint Germain and myself, has humbled me greatly. I know that Saint Germain appreciates your loving help as much as I do.

I must add to this list of acknowledgments Nancy Barton's name again for putting *A Legacy of Love* into its final template form for the printers. Through much laughter, great patience, and the burning of the midnight oil, you so dedicatedly brought it all together. Heavenly Father, as he does so often, sent you at the right time to see this project through in breakneck speed!

To all of you mentioned, and those not mentioned, who know of my gratitude for your presence in my life in small and large ways, I extend deepest gratitude. Because of this circle of love that has surrounded my work for the past 16 years, countless numbers of lives—on this side and in the spirit world—have been helped to progress and come closer to their real self and our Heavenly Father who has orchestrated all of our lives into one great concert of love.

Philip Burley
April 28, 2003, Phoenix, AZ

Contents

Preface in Two Parts

Part I

The Life of Philip Burley—A Synopsis

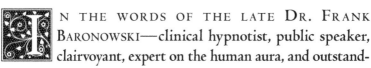N THE WORDS OF THE LATE DR. FRANK BARONOWSKI—clinical hypnotist, public speaker, clairvoyant, expert on the human aura, and outstanding radio host of "Mysteries Around Us" on KTAR, Phoenix, AZ, October 2001: "Can spirit voices on the other side have the ability ... to tap into certain individuals here [on earth] so that humanity might be helped? Yes! That's the kind of man that Philip Burley is. I'm looking at his aura, ladies and gentlemen ... He has a brilliant aura—an expansion of blue like I have never seen! But the thing that goes with it is that it's topped with a very fine line of gold. In my whole life I have only seen a fine line of gold around four other people! I've had audiences with Pope John and Sai Baba and all types of holy people. I am deeply impressed."

Philip Burley was born on Thanksgiving Day, November 23, 1939 in Fort Wayne, Indiana. His childhood was replete with bedside spirit visitations and nightly, conscious,

I

out-of-the-body experiences and travels into the spirit world to be with and learn from the Masters.

Concerned more with his relationship with God than his spiritual gifts, Philip has spent a lifetime in pursuit of God. For this reason many consider him as much mystic as medium. He credits his spiritual gifts as stemming from his quest and direct experiences with God, whom he calls his "Heavenly Father."

At the age of 47—after many years of struggling, searching, praying and having already had a broad array of enlightening and leading spiritual experiences—Saint Germain appeared and spoke audibly to Philip (a well-documented and tape recorded conversation) in Ephrata, Pennsylvania on July 5, 1987. Philip recalls it as "a most moving and unbelievable experience. Not one which I sought, but one that seemed to come by grace."

"There I sat, in awe, listening to the voice of Saint Germain as he spoke out loud to me so that anyone there could have heard him. As Germain entered the room, he powerfully intoned: 'This is Saint Germain and I come in the golden and purple light and from all that is holy. It is so great indeed that we can be with someone who is as dedicated as you are.'

Germain proceeded to speak to me intimately about my spiritual walk and instructed me on how to develop greater sensitivity in my mediumship: 'We must meet each other halfway, each doing his part.' He then told me most lovingly, 'If you love others as yourself—regardless of who they are, in spite of what they do or do not do—then that unconditional caring will draw me [Germain] so close to you that I will be permanently cemented into your aura and we will move together at all times.' In total, Saint Germain and I spoke for nearly thirty minutes on that occasion."

Two and one-half years—and many spiritual experiences later—Germain, without Philip's effort or prompting, began channeling through "medium-mystic" Philip's vocal cords to clients and gathered audiences across the country and from around the world. And the rest is history.

PART II

The Life and Times of Saint Germain

Philip Burley hosted the very popular radio show **The Inner View— Adventures in Spirit** *on KXAM, KFNX and VoiceAmerica.com from Phoenix, Arizona for a period of three years, 1999 - 2001.* **The Inner View** *was heard throughout the state of Arizona and around the world through the Internet.*

On these highly acclaimed shows Philip gave many talks on the spirit world and closely related topics. He also taught meditation and on many shows led his listeners into the reverie and benefits of this art. In addition, as a medium, Philip gave countless spiritual readings to call-in listeners and often spontaneously channeled the illustrious Saint Germain. "The man who never ages" [Saint Germain] also gave talks and spent very personal time in question and answer format with listeners who availed themselves, via phone, to this great master. The phones were always lit up while Philip and Saint Germain were on the air. So popular and in demand were their individual and combined talents.

The following is an excerpt from one such show and serves well as a partial and meaningful introduction to the work and talents of Philip Burley and the spiritual master, Comte de Saint Germain.

 ODAY I WILL BE SPEAKING ON *The Life and Times of Saint Germain,* which I am sure will be of great interest to you, and give you much needed insight into who Saint

Germain is and what great contribution he made to the political and spiritual progress of the world. Much of this information is not known by the general public because it is not actually written in our mainstream history books.

The Life and Times of Saint Germain: this title came to me as I ended last week's show, and Master Germain stepped up to my right, behind me, and said, "I would like you to speak on the 'life and times of myself.'" I didn't know what he meant. But before I sat down to compose the script for today's show, I went for about a 45-minute walk early in the morning purposely to think and reflect on Saint Germain's directive to write about him. No sooner had I started my walk when I realized that Saint Germain had come with me. In my usual mediumistic way, when not in trance, I could sense his presence around me as he dictated, bit by bit, just what he wanted me to speak on today specifically. When I got home, I hurriedly wrote down what Saint Germain told me and combined it with my own knowledge from obscure and mostly esoteric writings, some of which can be found in a museum in England.

Let me begin with "The Life and Times of Saint Germain."

Being a Bridge Between the Worlds

World history is replete with those individuals who had the ability to perceive dimensions beyond this earthly realm. Unknown experientially to the majority of humanity we, on earth, are constantly surrounded by the presence of spiritual beings. And the individuals I speak of, these sensitives, who could perceive the spirit world, knew by life experience, that the spirit world is real.

Whether they are called soothsayers, shamans, prophets, oracles, mystics, psychics, or mediums, they all served, and still serve, as bridges between the world of spirit and the world of flesh.

Depending upon a number of factors, including culture, level of education, degree of spiritual growth, belief system, and so on, so were the levels of spirit world contacted by these individuals of which I speak: the spiritually sensitive, yet superstitious, would likewise contact those in spirit (who had also been superstitious while on earth), further amplifying and perpetuating such superstitions and keeping erroneous belief systems alive. Still others among the world's sensitives were more evolved, and touched in with even higher realms, where pure truths were known, and in which superstition could not take root. Then there were, and are, all degrees in between these two extremes.

And of course, I have not included here, those dealing in witchcraft, black magic and voodoo, and the spirit world that perpetuates *these* kinds of beliefs and practices. Those of this ilk I would not place separately from the world's spiritually sensitive, but I would say that they rank in the lower echelons of spirit contact and manifestations, and enjoy their efforts not in the light, but in darkness.

Spiritual Influence throughout the Ages

Whatever the culture, whatever the level of spiritual development, whatever the truths perceived and perpetuated, the world has been greatly influenced, both to the good and bad, through the revelations of the spiritually sensitive or spiritually open individuals. Moses was one such individual who, through clairvoyance and clairaudience, communicated with God, and through materialization, received the 10 Commandments. Jesus was definitely among this group as he demonstrated amply his spiritual perception and gifts. And St. Paul, who followed him, began his life with Jesus after, through clairvoyance and clairaudience, he experienced Jesus in a blazing, blinding burst of light on the road to Damascus.

Paul, having gifts of the spirit, could then write, and even leave a record of the very kind and degree of one's experience with these gifts, as found in Chapter 13 in the Book of Corinthians of the New Testament. In fact, the whole Christian Bible is filled with manifestation after manifestation of spiritual phenomena from the appearance of angels to spirit communication, to the spirit writing on the wall in the Book of Daniel, to the turning of water into wine by Jesus Christ himself. This is but to mention a few examples.

Do we not know that Buddha, Mohammad, Zoroaster, Confucius, Lao Tzu, Swedenborg, Martin Luther, John Wesley, Joseph Smith, and countless other major and minor so-called religious leaders and founders—past and present day—were all overshadowed to varying degrees by spirits with these spirits' interest in perpetuating certain beliefs as truth, partial and/ or ultimate, based upon limited knowledge and experience? Jesus himself communicated with Moses and Elijah while some of his disciples watched on—as these two figures from Old Testament history materialized right before their eyes!

Each one of these religious founders and leaders, whether they knew it or not, or cared to admit it to their contemporaries or in their written records, was influenced by revelations from the spirit world which they, in part, combined with their own beliefs, cultural bents, level of education, both from life experience and formal education, and level of spiritual growth.

This leads me to say, therefore, that the human element in religious teachings abounds, and is no little reason for the great suffering in the mental and emotional clutches of some religious teachings. To what degree such teachings are really from God in many cases is highly questionable, if we contrast these teachings against the backdrop of God as a divine, unconditional, loving, most forgiving being.

Erasing the Boundaries

Into such a world came Saint Germain, a world centered upon and divided by religions internally and politics externally. As a mystic, Saint Germain knew directly of God's presence in himself. His approach to spirituality was centered upon God within first and upon spiritual phenomena second. He was a highly developed clairvoyant and clairaudient. But, over and above this, he was a man who loved individuals personally and humanity at large.

Arriving in a world that was greatly divided religiously and politically and struggling on many levels, Saint Germain came to change all of that. How? And where? According to esoteric writings, Saint Germain came to America and was present—with the signers of the Declaration of Independence at the site of the meeting, in Philadelphia. His appearance took place prior to the actual signing of the historical document. While commanding great attention and getting it, he spoke very enthusiastically and with much conviction that they must sign the Declaration. And what followed is history.

Having met with great success in a fledgling America, Germain returned to the other side of the Atlantic to duplicate the establishment of democracy in France and from there, one surmises, to the rest of Europe.

Before making this approach and appeal to the nobility of France, Saint Germain traveled all over Europe and England to the heads of state which, at that time, would have been called the noble class. Through these multiple visitations over enough periods of time, Saint Germain made himself known, and drew both attention and favor as he performed outstanding miracles. Accounts of some of these miracles can be found in preserved diaries of noble women who witnessed this adept's spiritual manifestations.

Germain executed amazing feats, demonstrating his spiritual ability as he appeared and disappeared out of and into thin air. He did a major materialization that turned an entire palace ballroom into a forest with grazing deer simply from a piece of deer horn and a twig from a tree, and some other elements. Down the center of the lavishly decorated room Germain materialized a long banquet table holding a sumptuous feast for the attending, amazed guests!

At other times, Saint Germain would suddenly arrive at the right time in the right place without being summoned, so as to step in and give aid or advice where needed at the state level or personal level. He literally predicted the coming of the French Revolution and the dissolution of the reign of kings in France if the nobility did not change their way of treating the masses with indifference, and allowing for a life of great suffering and poverty as the noble class lived and ruled in splendor.

Some may conclude that Saint Germain, in his mixing with the upper crust of society, did so because he was a social snob. That was not the case at all! It was a matter of wisdom. Who in those days had power to change things, but the tiny ruling class? They could influence change overnight. And they had the political power to do so. Their word, in fact, was law.

Teaching the Essence of God

Saint Germain, a spiritual master, knew the full reality of the effects he was trying to bring. He knew well, for example, from life experience, that there was but one God who was accessible to all, regardless of their social or economical circumstances. He also knew that religion held sway over the lives of millions of people in Europe and England as the clergy sought, by self-justifying teachings, to stand between God and each individual.

Germain—as Jesus in his day—knew that such an arrangement was not pleasing to God. His experience, again like that of Jesus, taught him that God lived in each being. Germain's own spiritual life and personal relation with God taught him that *no one* had the right to determine another's relationship with God. He might have said that that relationship was a private and sacred one, even as a marriage between a man and woman is private and sacred. This being the foundation and pivotal point of all creation to a man of Germain's spiritual experience and stature was an undeniable and fundamental truth and right of every human being.

You see, it was not to the advantage of either the state or the church of that day to have an awakening or enlightenment coming to the masses. Democracy, based directly upon each individual's inalienable rights, could thwart the rule of the many by a few, as each one awoke to his own God-given responsibility for self and direct personal relationship with the living God.

In the end, it was the lack of appreciation and recognition of the rights of all human beings as denied—directly or indirectly—by the royals of England that ultimately caused the first exodus from England, and the establishment of a land of democracy—a land where no one held sway over another's life, either politically or religiously.

Ringing the Bell of Freedom

Saint Germain, therefore, sought first to appeal to the noble classes. Again, because it was they who could change the course of human history in Europe. For up to that point in the evolution of humanity, democracy in Europe had never existed. And in order for man to find and know God, man needed the freedom that democracy allowed to pursue, with all his heart, a personal relationship with God. Saint Germain knew all of this well, and wanted everyone else to know, and be free to fulfill the divine ideal of marriage between man and God. It was to this end he was working, and not to gain favor or favoritism with the ruling class.

The French Revolution, as a result of the monarchy and the political cronies around them not listening, not caring, brought on their own demise. And with the Revolution the establishment of modern-day democracy in Europe and England ultimately came to pass.

In examining the life of Germain through historical writings and my own experience with him over 13 years [at the time this program aired], it's easy to conclude that this man did not come in the context of something purely spiritual or religious. He did not come to display messianic capabilities to sway the masses to follow him by signs and wonders, by public speeches against organized government or religion. Rather, he came with great love for all people, the highest of high "religions." As I said, Germain did not come to change the order of things, or to *displace* the rulership of the land, but to get these same people to see the light and understand that their duty was to evolve in truth and love, to bring physical and spiritual freedom to all under their command, and to spread this freedom. They could not do it. They *did* not do it! And revolution, including the demise of the rulers, took place just as Germain had predicted, according to factual, historical writings.

As a champion of individual human freedom, based upon universal and personal care and love, Saint Germain sought and continues to seek this for each human being. He still does not seek either a messianic role or a following, but admonishes each one to pursue the inner path of self-discovery and mastery to ultimately discover and reveal God within. Over and over, he eschews dependency upon another person's idea of God, telling us not to leave such choices up to another, but rather to meet God face-to-face in ourselves. He admonishes us to know from direct experiences who God is and who we are.

In the climate of democracy, a growing form of government around the world, such independent and individual pursuit of God is made possible. Otherwise, in many prior forms of government throughout the world, and even some still remaining, each of us would be under the dictatorship of a few who would tell the majority, whom, what, where, and when to worship or not to worship. To not conform to such dictates from on high could result in imprisonment or death.

From what I've shared with you in this discourse, it becomes obvious that we have Saint Germain, and others like him from the world of spirit, to thank for their undying efforts in trying to bring political and spiritual freedom to planet earth, through the establishment of democracy. Set in this context, our awareness of both the universality and multi-dimensional nature of Saint Germain is considerably expanded. And our appreciation greatly increased. He is a man of great character, strong will, and unconditional love, combined with great spiritual astuteness and sensitivity, who has influenced the world toward significant progress and hope.

Without God sending such noble and far-sighted spiritual masters to earth, life here could not be nearly as advanced as it is. It is highly possible that we could still be living in the dark ages without their monumental influence. The work of Saint Germain and thousands of other great masters from Spirit continues in many forms, many unknown by man on earth. Through the avenue of trance channeling on a radio program like *The Inner View: Adventures in Spirit,* which Saint Germain inspired to come into being, he continues in part with the work he started: helping man to become free in God.

Introduction

HE VOLUME YOU HOLD IN YOUR HANDS is a rare book. It may look plain and simple, but its contents are moving and mighty. Such is the presence and power of its author, Saint Germain.

For the past 16 years he has been my constant companion and guide along with three other spirit guides who participate in the wonderful and marvelous adventure of my mediumship.

Included in this edition of *A Legacy of Love With Saint Germain* are representative examples of the Master's words of wisdom. It was very thoughtfully prepared for the occasion of *The Clear Light of God Wesak Celebration 2003* and in remembrance of his appearance on Mount Shasta 73 years ago this year to Mr. Guy Ballard. That appearance is well chronicled in Ballard's world famous book, *The Unveiled Mysteries.*

It was Ballard's book, in large part, which set me off on a journey with Saint Germain and transformed my life into one of the most unbelievable, mysterious and spiritually elevating experiences possible.

I am eternally in Saint Germain's debt, along with my other guides and teachers, for getting my attention and leading the way in a mission filled with endless and often unfathomable blessings.

As most honest spiritual masters of the gift of medium-ship will tell you, "It is not easy doing what I do." I echo that classical comment. "It is not easy to do what I do." Good mediumship is an art—which if entered into correctly, for maximum, authentic demonstration of the gift to clients or sitters—one has to forget self and be a pure, unattached channel for Spirit.

One of the most famous English mediums of the 20th Century, Eileen Garrett, doubted her gift many times, even to her dying day. It is because a true medium is a funnel, detached from *the process* as Spirit uses you as they would when using a telephone. In other words, using that now well-worn phrase, "The medium is *not* the message!"

I, Philip Burley would add, "No, I am not the message, I am the *passage*." So to do what I do, "I" have to get out of the way so that the spirit world can bring through to earth, pure, unadulterated messages from on high! The less the medium is present, in other words—without ego attachment, without concern for the outcome—the better they are for Spirit's use.

In the midst of preparing what you are about to read, as I scurried among transcripts strewn across my living room floor, I grew weary from the process of picking out just which words of Saint Germain, spoken through me on this or that occasion, would be best suited for this book. To take a well-needed break, I went out on our patio to lie on a chaise lounge to bask and rest in the April, Arizona afternoon sun. I had intended to rest but a few minutes and then return to the task at hand.

Not realizing how really tired I was, I drifted off into my usual mediumistic reverie—a place somewhere between not completely awake and not completely asleep. It felt good to let go for a few moments and feel my humanness and bodily limitations. Such humbling experiences keep me grounded in the reality that I am just a passageway for Spirit. I am the means and not the end. How sweet it was to lie there in this altered state, like a baby waiting to be held in the arms of Heaven.

As I had done countless times in my life, starting at a very young age, I passed into a state of being that always appears as limitless light and a peace beyond earthly experience. No sooner had I come into this very familiar "space" when Saint Germain suddenly appeared to my right with a most welcoming and warm smile on his face. I was so happy! I had been asking him to appear and give me support and encouragement in the daunting responsibility of compiling his words for "our" appearance at the Wesak Festival at Mount Shasta.

He was unusually warm and supportive whereas often, while never stern or commanding, he is most often quite serious and dignified looking. It was his purple attire that first signaled he was there. He wore a purple cape made of a material that, at close inspection, looked like finely spun wool. I could not see the garment he wore under it. The aura around him was totally made of love and flowed into me as a healing balm while he spoke to me.

I was so pleased that he had come to me in this way. Usually I experience him as a voice beside me or behind me during my mediumship work. At times he has come in sleeping dreams. Then, too, he will sometimes appear in front of me, if the need arises, and speak while pacing or moving about, especially when I am giving spiritual readings to my clients.

However, today he was closer than ever and more "real" than any other time I had seen him either with my physical or spiritual sight. This comforted me and gave me greater, undeniable reassurance that Saint Germain lived, cared, and had heard my call!

To make a long story short, Saint Germain reassured me that he was happy with my work and that I would be guided in the assembling of *A Legacy of Love With Saint Germain.* Additionally, he gave me confidence in my mediumship, for the umpteenth time, and that all would go well in our "visit" together at Mount Shasta.

With all that said, combined with his most personal emanation of love toward me, he turned and disappeared into the world of the invisibles. At that point I got up, so refreshed, so inspired and infinitely grateful for all my spiritual guides and teachers, especially Saint Germain, and for my Heavenly Father who had sent them.

It is in this context that I make *A Legacy of Love With Saint Germain* available to the public. And I do so with great joy and the anticipation that each one who reads it will find precious, multi-faceted gems of wisdom and healing dew drops of love throughout its pages.

Philip Burley
April 20, 2003
Phoenix, Arizona

Part One

Scaling the Summit ~ Mount Shasta Wesak Festival

OOD EVENING. THIS IS SAINT GERMAIN.

"The life that's not investigated," someone wrote in human history, "is not worth living." Indeed, unless you stop and really look at your very own personal life you're not going to be able to obtain the level of awareness or enlightenment that you could otherwise.

As long as you identify with your body, with your name, with your birthday, your thoughts, feelings and mind as being *you*, when I tell you that they *are not* you, you will not find your true self. I'm not saying you shouldn't identify with these aspects of your earthly life *at all*. I am saying that while you have to carry out your life here on earth as a unique individual—even if it's only transitory or as a part of some cosmic movie or dream—don't *attach* yourself to anything on earth. Attach yourself to God. I repeat: as long as you identify with those things I just mentioned as *yourself*, then you are going to be kept from knowing who you *really* are, which is beyond your earthly identity.

Self-Mastery and the I AM Presence

Now I, Saint Germain, am a spiritual being. I have realized many of the things that Philip has talked about; otherwise, I could not take him to the level to which he is now going. Without my assistance and without that kind of rapport, it would not be possible for him to transcend to a higher level that he spoke of earlier—about coming to perceive life from the super-conscious mind and beyond into cosmic-consciousness.

It is from this vantage point that one can "know" just who they are and what the **I AM** is. It is from this higher perspective or state of mind that I, Saint Germain, am able to do what I do as a spiritual master and be who **I AM**.

Because I worked at self-mastery and obtained it, I am called a master. Resultantly, I have an awareness, a considerable awareness, of what it is to reach and exist in a highly expanded state of consciousness. It is not theory to me. Otherwise I could not have achieved self-mastery nor could I teach about it, you see.

When I was on earth, most of you know I performed many so-called "miracles." You cannot do that simply by being an ordinary person. You have to transcend into that part of yourself where the magic is, where the divine spark is. And you have to consciously, over time and by the grace of God, release that *divine power* within you and streaming through you at all times, to perform such so-called miracles.

Because of my entire life experience on earth and here in the spirit world, I am able to go between the Golden Path (the royal path to God) and the lesser paths. Due to full self-mastery, I'm equipped to come to you this way by lowering my energies, or I can soar ever higher and higher into the very heart and mind of God, the ever-present, **I AM Presence.**

Coming to Earth—Then and Now

As a spiritual master I am able to come to you through this instrument and speak on an endless number of topics—to inspire you, to teach you, to answer your questions and much more. Afterwards, I will return to engage my energies in the work that I carry on in the spirit world. Back and forth, back and forth we masters go to carry on our appointed calling of working between heaven and earth for the sole purpose of helping others.

Through the gift of channeling, I am able come to you, to talk about the higher reality within yourself, make pronouncements, give guidance, tell you what it's like here in spirit and then return to the role I play in the world of spirit—all with the ease of a thought.

While I am Saint Germain, the individual you know, I have also alluded to the fact that I am a cosmic being who is capable of playing many roles. But my essential character, my essential reality, is that I am the being whom you call Saint Germain. I am not someone in the guise of Saint Germain. I am Saint Germain.

I must add that it is my influence, and those who work with me on this side, who have made these gatherings possible, who have been, as it were, the voice of reason and love crying out to assemble a group like this for the express purpose of going to Mount Shasta where I first appeared some 73 years ago.

So you have many questions about that reality, that is, why now, and how is this taking place, and what will happen there, and what is the purpose of it all? And over the weeks I shall open the doorway to allow you to ask some of those questions. To the best of my ability I will provide you with the answers you seek.

What you don't know right now is that for Philip to appear there, we wanted to, as does any person who's working with a fine instrument, "tune him up." We wanted to, as it were, tighten the strings and make sure that he is properly strung [like a violin] in order for us to use him. And so we are using these meetings to provide an opportunity to enhance our use of him.

The more you pray for my manifestation through him, the more energy will be available for me to do that. But as you have observed him over the years, our relationship does not vary; his dedication to my coming and doing this work through him, has not changed. In fact, he is more dedicated now than ever before.

Manifesting Ever More Greatly

Now for those of you who may think that this is just Philip's consciousness speaking through Philip, it is not so. There is a portion of him present. For that reason, we have inspired him to get more out of the way through seeking a deeper trance state—but the reality is, I am here behind him and **I AM** "pouring" myself into him. Over the years there have been those of you who are clairvoyant who have seen me transfigure over him, or have seen the emanation of the golden and purple light in which I come to you.

You see, we would like to remove him more so we can manifest more fully. Not because we're ambitious to occupy his precious body, but because we want to make it possible for more and more people to know and to understand that there *is* life after death, that they may be liberated from fear, for want of information. Using him, even more fully than we are now, gives him and us that opportunity.

Concepts of Life and Death

And speaking of "death," man should not be afraid to live because he's going to die! He should be able to be free and happy to live, knowing that *he* never dies. *He* only makes transition. With the fear of death out of the way, he may use the greater portion of his energies on bettering himself for that transition, as opposed to wasting time on ideas of heaven and hell, and upon death.

You know, life is for living. And you cannot live life unless you "live." And living means taking chances. It means taking risks. It means growing into courage to do the things that you don't particularly want to do or like to do, but still you do them because you understand their value, even if it is only the value of challenging yourself. So "dare to fail!" That was my motto: "Dare to fail!" Because in *daring to fail,* you will know what it feels like to be on the brink of failure, and find within yourself resources you never knew you had, by which you will also learn how to rescue yourself. After all, to dare to fail is only a thought. And once you catch the

25

secret of how *not* to fail, you will realize the secret is to stop thinking about failure and only think success!

The truth is that you draw to yourself what you are. Because the instrument I am speaking through is one who from childhood dedicated himself to experiencing spirit and communing with us, we could come to him regularly, teach him and ultimately use him for the purpose he is presently manifesting before you this very moment.

Ever Surrender

It was within Philip Burley's God-given personality and character to pursue such an end. In the latter years it is all that he has thought of, focusing his entire life upon being a mediumistic bridge for Saint Germain and others to cross to planet earth over the past 16 years. By this fortunate and blessed means we have served the countless numbers of waiting and spiritually hungry souls as we have. What he focused upon and practiced, with all due diligence, he has become. This is the true and eternal path to self-mastery. It is how you become all that you become and draw to yourself what you are!

Regarding Philip's example, I admonish all of you who have high ideals, whatever they may be, to not give up on them. Do not think that because something has not yet happened that it can't happen. Miracles do happen. But they happen through the practical reality of applying oneself, of having the utmost perseverance to make one's ideal come to pass. Additionally, whether you feel as if you are struggling or grappling with difficult things, whatever they may be—personal, in your business life, or with another human being—be very patient. In summary, feed your mind only thoughts of success, thoughts of progress, thoughts of overcoming and realize your ideals while maintaining supreme patience! Then surrender everything to God!

The Essence of You

Going back to what I was saying originally, it all has to do with finding God within—the great **I AM**. The way to do that is when you are thinking, *think* about your thinking. Step back from it. Even in the midst of your anger, ask yourself, "Is this something I put on, or am I actually angry in my core self?" When you start to think that way, you will realize that at core you are not *really* angry. Through such introspection, via your reasoning, you transcend into that place within your *eternal, higher self* where only peace prevails. And at that point, you'll realize that with reasoning, you're not feeling the anger. Consequently, you will realize that anger is something you have put on, but it's not your essential nature. Your essential nature is joy and peace and will never change. This too is the essential nature of God and it is called "bliss." It will never change.

If God's essential nature were to change, the balance of the entire cosmos would be undone and everything destroyed. How can God, the major core energy—the only source of all life—alter in some way and not alter all of life? No, God is that steady, steady stream of divine love pouring out of a reservoir of limitless capacity, who is ever giving his energy for the purpose of fulfilling his own dream, his own ideal. There is literally and absolutely no end to this reality with God. It is in this way that God is the Grand Master of us all. By steadfast focus—out of the stream of the cosmic-consciousness and love that he is—he created all of life and realized his ideal.

When you tap into your eternal, essential nature, then you become an individual who is boundless, who can also make miracles happen and realize your ideals. I would recommend, however, that you not try too hard at making your ideas into reality, for it is God who is acting through you that completes the process. As you realize this eternal truth and willingly *surrender* yourself to him, he will animate you more fully and work through you all day long. He is already operating in you. He always has been. Awareness of and surrender to this fact greatly increases God's opportunity to manifest and act through your life. It is the greatest, single secret to self-mastery. Learn to let go, and let God!

The analogy of the hand in the glove is not quite appropriate, but it is close. As you accept God putting you on his hand, be humble, receptive, open, without concepts of what should happen or how it should happen, and then the force of God within you will take over and make your ideals into reality.

God—the Composer, the Conductor

Some of you are already living a life of surrender to God and you are finding, resultantly, that life just seems to go more and more smoothly. That is, things happen in the right time and in the right way. And when they don't, you have learned that it's because they're not supposed to.

Eventually we learn that there is a master musical score sheet that God is using to orchestrate our existence. He knows the notes on the page and he knows how to conduct you to play the right tune. He is the one holding the baton, conducting the concerto of your life.

I am so pleased to have you and your spiritual guides and teachers joining in and cooperating with this work of Saint Germain. As you can imagine, or if you can see clairvoyantly, I am more than just Saint Germain. There are many thousands and thousands behind this work on spirit side, whose lives and the lives of their counterparts on earth you are helping by your participation with this instrument of Philip Burley.

Through your participation in this work, you are going to afford many people the opportunity to approach a higher path, a path not so encumbered by complexities of thought, by circuitous concepts and thinking. For the path—the Golden Path—that you and I are on, goes directly to the *top* of the Mountain, and not *around and around*. This is what Saint Germain, gathered hosts, Philip Burley, and those who work with him on earth are ultimately about. This is what I was about in my visit to Mount Shasta in the early years of the last century. My aim and purpose remains the same: to go for the top of the Mountain and bring with me as many as are able to understand and walk the upper path to true, human freedom in God. For this reason alone, Mount Shasta serves as a majestic and perfect symbol for the work we do together. Let us climb together and let us be climbing now!

The Conveyance of the Violet Light

At this point, I would like you to get very quiet, very still, that I may pervade this room with the Violet Light and with the presence of my many helpers here in the spirit world.

29

Feel my presence with you. Feel all of our presence with you. In this great silence, I do bring the Violet Light. It is for your awakening. It is for your healing. It is for new vision. It is my gift to you on this wonderful spiritual eve. I bless you with it always as I take my leave. My love is always with you.

This is Saint Germain. God bless you.

DISCOURSE TWO

True Enlightenment

OOD EVENING. THIS IS SAINT GERMAIN.

God is light; there's not a trace of darkness in him.
I love this reality! Who would choose darkness over light, if
they could feel the all-enveloping reality of the love of God?

I come from that sphere where there is perpetual sunshine.
It is a place where God's love shines forth endlessly, abundantly,
universally. And we bask in it, night and day of your earthly
time. Does that not make you long to go home to God?

This is a realm beyond the realms written in your books
on earth. It is beyond your comprehension. And yet, your soul
partakes of it perpetually. Otherwise, you could not be alive
or exist, as God's being is manifest in your being. Since God
is, you are.

Your awareness is possible because of God's ever-present
heart beat and mindfulness within you. Your intelligence—
that is the ability to discern one thing from another, to

label things, to comprehend things—is possible because God's intelligence is ever flowing through you. It is an ever-manifesting electrical current of love and light that is the Source of all life.

And so I come to bathe you in that love and light, by raising your understanding of just where I come from and where you are headed, as you focus upon the reality of God within.

Beloved ones, you will increasingly awaken to that warm, brilliant, blinding, all-encompassing light within yourself. It is shining there now. You have but to open the windows of your understanding to dispel the ignorance which blocks out that brilliant light.

When that light comes in fully and completely, it floods your whole being with all that it is. And therefore, in a moment of that experience, there comes eternal understanding—comprehension beyond any level you have ever aspired to or realized. Then you know yourself as you are known by God and us. The darkness of ignorance that covers the window of understanding is removed from you by the inclusion of this magnificent light, and you see things as they are. You know all things as you tap into endless universal consciousness and the emanation of God's thought flows unhindered and fully into yours. This is how true enlightenment is made manifest.

Living in the Now

At this level of comprehension, the past, the present and the future are all seen at once. Therefore, in this cosmic thought, there is no time. And because we see both cause and effect in the portrayal of the past, present and future, we see suffering as one with joy. For it is through the ebb and flow of life

experience—between these two extremes of joy and suffering—
that the past and the present takes place, and the end results
that our Heavenly Father was seeking to achieve are achieved.

Remember that there are, therefore, no mistakes. There is
only the passage of what you call time. But it is all happening
now. That is why we talk about living in the now. The second
that I am speaking is now gone, and I am already in the future.
And so it is now. And now. And now.

It is only in your mind that you think there is such a thing
as viewing the past, or looking toward the future. The past is
now, the present is now, and the future is now. Because God
knows all three simultaneously, he planned the beginning, the
middle, and the end of all things as they flow through their
cycles of life. Therefore, for God—being omniscient and
omnipresent—there is only now.

I drive home this point because as you are aspiring to
achieve higher and higher meditation techniques and benefits,
you will increasingly understand that as you become ever so
still, ever so peaceful, you are within yourself, coming more
and more into the presence of the living God right within you!
You will, as it were, come to live ever more in the now. You
will see life as God sees life. For once that flood of light that
is God is opened into you, you are never the same. You never
look at life in the same way. It is not only a mental effect, it
is a physiological effect in which every atom of your being is
touched by this light and, therefore, transformed.

Being Patience Itself

The summit of the Mountain of Life must be approached care-
fully, cautiously, so that you do not too quickly overwhelm your

being with the fullness of this light and do damage to yourself. Too much awareness too soon, and your mind, in terms of the physiological, spiritual, chemical, electrical elements, will be overburdened and burned out. Therefore, let your mantra be first that of *patience*. "I am patience itself. I am patience itself. I am patience itself." And trust your own Inner Intelligence to lead you where you need to go. Stay in that place in your journey upward, for Divine Intelligence is all-wise; it is taking you through ever higher and higher plateaus of your life and self-realization. It never removes its awareness from you, for its awareness is centered in you, for you.

You are forever broadcasting your reality. Yes, even as a television station broadcasts its reality, you are forever emanating an energy that is directly connected to the intelligence of God, and God's intelligence is connected directly to you in you. The entire design of your life is laid out by the Grand Architect. He is the most skillful, patient, wise, and loving artist, friend, and parent that you could ever want. And your life is completely in his hands.

My love follows you. This is Saint Germain.

DISCOURSE THREE

The Hallmark of Your Life

THIS IS SAINT GERMAIN. GOD BLESS YOU.

I know that you are happy to hear me come through my medium, and I am sending special energies to you that will stay with you for the next three days. Focus upon my name and see that name enveloped in the Violet Light, and I shall be there to impart uplifting energies to help you come into a more concrete vision for yourself.

You are born with a mission. Some people are born not knowing that their karmic reality is such that they do not have the privilege of being so aware. You are being divinely guided, and always have been, even in the low times.

Philip spoke at length about the necessity of finding greater self-confidence. Self-confidence is not something we can manufacture. It is not something we can conjure up. True self-confidence comes from seeing ourselves in the fulfillment of our life's work. If you cannot see yourself acting in your mission, if you cannot see it to some extent in your mind's eye, then you will lack enthusiasm and self-confidence.

Therefore, go inside and look at your interior self. Eighty percent or more of your meditation time should be spent in self-examination. This does not mean in morbid introspection. It means to look into your heart. The spiritual heart, unbeknownst to most, does not lie over the physical heart. The spiritual heart lies about one inch to the right of the physical heart. So, when you are in meditation, go into that spiritual part of yourself, and examine it objectively, even as if you were looking at someone else. Particularly, look at your motives and examine your own heart, asking yourself, "Who am I?"

The Circuitry of God's Love

When you finally observe and deduce that you, too, are God, then you will stop wrestling with self-doubt. God lives in each individual, literally! As I have said many times, without his energies we could not exist. God's energies are ever circulating through us which makes it possible for us to "be." It is his existence that makes our existence possible. No matter how perfect a light bulb—even with its filament intact—unless electricity flowed through it from an outside source, there would be no illumination. It is as the energy or electricity flows through the bulb that the bulb fulfills its purpose by lighting up.

In the same way, the circuit of God's loving energy is ever-flowing through us, which gives us life, "lights" us up like the bulb, and makes our existence as an animated being possible.

How much of the brightness of God's presence in us can be manifested depends upon our capacity to love. The more we practice love, the more opportunity is there to expand our capacity to love. The goal from Heavenly Father's perspective and practice is to love more and more people, and to love them ever more deeply.

When you look into your heart, look at the things that you really love in life, the things that make you most happy. What things do you find most soul-satisfying? As you look objectively and deeply into your heart you will find those soul-satisfying things spelled out in general terms, and later in specific terms, your life's mission.

God speaks to us *through* us, and he speaks from within the human heart. The human spiritual heart is the true and eternal heart of man. Through our spiritual heart we discern the truth of things and the spiritual heart therefore functions as the true "mind" of man. In the human brain there is cognizing, but it is in the human [spiritual] heart that there is the realization of God.

Unveiling Your Real Self

So take the time to observe yourself. Give yourself that time! Do not worry about the length of meditation as much as the quality of the meditation. As you follow my advice, many things will dawn in your consciousness for you to see that you do not now see. Your spiritual guides and teachers will come and help you work correctly with your inner self-discoveries. Most especially will Quan Yin—this lovely, lovely Master Teacher, who loves you so much and who has been working through your energies for many years—she will help you see your real self and make it dominant in your life.

"The proof is in the pudding" they say. In this case, that means if you will apply what Saint Germain has told you, it will be a hallmark in your life for the advancement to your higher and higher self. Actually, this process of examining self while in meditation should be a lifetime experience through which your real self is unveiled and your old false self dies away.

It is what we do in life, in part, that is important, but what is more important than the outer activity is why we do what we do. There are those who serve in many, many capacities in this world, but have no like for it. They have no affection for the people whom they serve. Their motive is not one of the highest level. But he who serves and loves and cares for the one he is serving, is the individual who will be spiritually elevated within.

The Pure Essence of His Purpose

So, take heart, dear one. When you look at yourself do not look at the downside. When you look at others, do not look at their shortcomings. Think of them as you, and love them as you would want to be loved.

If you will use this kind of self examination over time, you will find an exceeding increase in your own proper self love. Out of that will emerge the ability to master and guide your energies toward the right ends. It is our observation in the spiritual world that the masses of people don't have a clue about purpose, and are just living randomly from day to day. Yet look at the universe; it is very purposeful! It is ever moving toward the fulfillment of its essential purpose, and there is among all things within the universe, order.

When we do not have this order in our lives, it means that God is not the center. There truly is no center to life unless God is the center. How you know God, how you experience God, is through your individual path. No one can say to you that God is this or God is that. Since all things come from God, God is everything. There is nothing in which God does not exist. But you will meet that reality according to your own personality and life experience, and God will be as real to you as to anyone who experiences that reality.

Not to speak in parables or riddles, but this is the day in which God is peeling back the layers of falsehood to reveal the core truth, the true, pure essence of his purpose in the creation of all things, and most importantly, in the creation of humanity.

Now, as our time has come to an end, I am going to bid you farewell, but I leave with you my love and the love of those in the spiritual world who love you more than you love yourself. Remember this: there are many things from many angles we could say to you. Because of the limitation of time and also because everything must come in the right order at the right time, we cannot say everything. But know confidently that you are on the right path. You are being divinely guided, and if you will listen to that inner voice and be consistent with it, you will come to the right ends and you will be very happy that you listened when you did.

God bless you. This is Saint Germain.

Multi-Faceted You

THIS IS SAINT GERMAIN. I come with a heart filled with love and appreciation.

If we know God's presence by experience within us, there is no greater knowledge than this. And how wonderful that through this inner experience we are able to laugh and cry with God. This whole extremity and gamut of God's emotions are your emotions.

You want to know God? Know yourself. You are the offspring, the direct energy of the living God. Therefore, your character, your nature, your life are eternal. Your nature is precisely like his; and the range of emotions is the same as his. When you are sad, do not think that God feels differently. He is expressing through you. When you are filled with joy that causes you to burst into song or laughter, that is God in you expressing through you.

But this does not mean that God is just some kind of energy. No, indeed not. These manifestations are the personal, intimate manifestations of God. When you hear birds singing, it is not just some electrical, chemical, atomic energy manifesting in you and outside of you. It is God singing. When I speak thusly, I am so moved by the very presence of God that is in all of us. And so, you have all cried in moments of great joy or sadness, and you have also held yourself in those moments, either in your mind or with the very arms you possess.

Some will say, this is a silly idea. Why does God have to hold himself? Why would God have to express himself overtly to have all this joy? And I would reply, "Why does the eye have to see things in order to know that it sees? To be utilized?" Because it is through this dynamic of God's being—just being; looking overtly into the reflection of what he is in all things, including you—that he then becomes aware of himself, and becomes filled with bliss.

That's why we say, "I am being, awareness, bliss." Tonight, [in the meditation just prior] you focused upon the smoke rising from the incense. There you were just *being* and being quiet. But while being quiet, you became *aware* of the smoke before you; how it curly-cued; how it moved with the air; how it was silent; how its fragrance filled your nose; how you became more calm emulating its calmness or *bliss*.

So it is with God. When he contemplates the earth—this beautiful gem floating through space—what a glorious view! What great comfort he has, and great pride, from having created such a beautiful, beautiful planet. Of course, he can, at any moment, look at all the other planets, but Mother Earth is his pride and joy.

In this way within God's being, through consciousness or awareness, he sees himself reflected and experiences great joy and feels blissful resultantly. I say that it is all so gloriously beautiful!

The Launch Pad of Life Lessons

Here on this side in the world of spirit, standing around me tonight, are ringed those individuals who not long ago departed from this earth plane, via the Columbia [space shuttle]. [Saturday, February 1, 2003.]

You are the first among earthlings to have them greet you from this side. Why? Because this is a holy place. And they wanted to commemorate their departure with individuals who could appreciate the *full* spectrum of life, with those who are not mourning them, but can celebrate the glorious way in which they took their leave of Mother Earth.

Death was but a small price to pay for all that they realized and are realizing now. They are among the heroes and heroines here, having given their life for a high cause; their motives were so pure. And so I'm ringed by them tonight, and with the Master Jesus.

They are here also because you are going to Mount Shasta. We, from the spirit world, are making a proclamation about this event and this gentleman I am speaking through: it is a new time; and all the things that are happening worldwide are a part of God's great plan, including what is happening here this very moment.

It is all closely interwoven. It is all closely orchestrated by God. There is nothing happening that is not God's doing. Nothing. Your little heart beating, the water that comes forth to moisten your eyes. The movement of the food through your body. Every electron, every atom are under God's observation. And all things are working together, that he may have fun. That he may have joy. That he may have bliss. That his ideal and will may be fulfilled. But he also wants to endlessly teach you, and thus teach himself, who exists in you, the lessons of life.

God's multi-faceted nature is expressed through all of humanity. Each of you represents one facet of the billion billion-faceted jewel that God is. Isn't that beautiful? [**Yes.**] Therefore, each of you partakes of the light of God, and you reflect God, and you partake of and participate in the whole reality of God.

Each facet by the jeweler is what...? *Polished individually.* He doesn't do three or four at a time. He polishes one facet at a time. And so *each* of you must learn your lessons as God seeks to polish you personally with the abrasion of his most loving, cosmic grinding and polishing stone called life experience.

So these illustrative astronauts—standing behind Philip and me this moment—have learned their lessons through their recent departure from planet earth and through what they are learning here in the spirit world. Heavenly Father has polished them well. Consequently, they shine so very brilliantly in the world of spirit in this multi-faceted being called God. Isn't it beautiful? [**Yes.**] Glorious!

Reaching the Summit of Life

Mount Shasta represents the *Mountain of Life.* That's why I appeared there. So when you go there, remember me when you look at the peak of Mount Shasta. For that is where I look. That is my goal on the *Mountain of Life.* I do not want to remain in the *Valley of Life*, I want to go for the *Summit of Life!* That is where God shines brightest. It's a great symbol, is it not? [**Yes.**]

And so these wonderful, wonderful astronauts, who are smiling behind me, *did* climb the Summit of Life as they went out in a blaze of glory. And now they fully understand. Don't let anyone else ever tell you differently.

While others are crying on earth, they bemoan something that is not missing. No one died. Only their bodies perished. They are here in spirit more alive than you are! Now these travelers of outer and *inner* space can see cause *and* effect. And, therefore, are so liberated from the fear of life and death.

Before they passed into this arena—in that speeding space ship toward their departure, their transition into pure spirit life—they saw this side already. Their spiritual senses were opened. We allowed it, that they could come over, not in fear, but in anticipation and joy.

This part of life none of you know because on earth death is portrayed as something to fear. No, those who walk bravely toward death do not even see or feel death. They only see the light and feel its eternal, loving embrace. That is a hidden secret from earthly eyes and experiential knowledge, my dear friends.

I'm so happy to come to you tonight, to be here with you to bring this message. It is *not* a solemn time, but a time of rejoicing. We celebrate each one's arrival in this Land of Love and supreme human freedom.

Fortunately or unfortunately, I can leave, and yet you have to stay here. Many on this side envy you because you know that you are a facet of God. When they were on earth, many of them did not know that. You understand that life's struggles are to polish you; many of them did not know that. You can look upon suffering as opportunity, when they did not. And most of you are young enough that you have time to stand still and bask in the love and glory of the Father, in suffering and in joy, and be fully polished before you come here.

Understanding the Essence of Transition

I, Saint Germain, am very, very filled with pathos tonight. My tears are more because I feel the love of God for, in, and with you. And yet, you still have to climb the Mountain further to get the full, full experience of what is possible in this earthly life. In part, this makes me sad.

Secondly, I cry because on earth, due to ignorance, so many bemoan transition. I do not even like the word "death." I call it "transition." Let us abolish its use from the face of the earth—the word "death." Let us not allow it to be said. But let us replace it, wherever we go, with the word "transition."

Say it with me. Transition. [**Transition.**] Isn't that positive? [**Yes.**] Say the word "death," and see how that feels. Death. [**Death.**] Transition. [**Transition**] Transition. [**Transition.**] Do not think of death. Think of transition.

We are here together, you and I, and the newly arrived space travelers. We can smile and rejoice at their departure, whereas in the world many—who do not know of a more glorious life beyond earth in the Realms of Light—will think we are insensitive and should not be so happy but mourn them. Few are more sensitive than I am when it comes to these things. And yet, I do not cry because they made transition. "Rejoice!" For the astronauts have been born into a life far more enlightening, beautiful and free than any life on earth. It was their time!

Know—*know*—my love always, always follows you. God bless you. This is Saint Germain.

DISCOURSE FIVE

Love is the Reigning Principle

[Saint Germain's voice is filled with laughter as he comes in saying...]

AM HERE. I AM SO HAPPY TO BE WITH YOU TODAY. I am so joyful to be here with you. As I said to Philip, which occasioned this meeting, we need more of the contemporary things coming from heaven if we're going to publish a book. I am a contemporary being, living now. You might have some idea that I'm just an old man somewhere in a broken down house in the spirit world. Or some old-fashioned house. I have all the latest gadgets if I want them. But I'm hardly ever home. So I have little need for anything except this purple robe that I am wearing, and this band of gold all around me.

I'd like to place this occasion in the hands of the Father as I open with a prayer.

49

Our beloved Father,

Thou art the source of all life. And without thee, there would be no life. This laughter with which I come in to this circle is Your laughter. Even as the tears which we cry here are your tears.

We celebrate the great broadness of thyself, for thou art limitless love, limitless knowledge and understanding. And thy will is a perfect will. Nothing happens outside of thy observance. And it is not out of some formality, Father, that I begin this channeling occasion with this wonderful group of people. But it is because I know the source of my life, the source of my energy is from thee. Thou hast found favor with me, and thou hast given me the pleasure and privilege of entering into the human world on the face of Mother Earth again and again to bring thy children home to thee. How much I celebrate thee, Father! Almighty God. Thy love excels my understanding, goes beyond my comprehension, but touches me so personally that I do know that thou art mine, and I am thine.

It is this kind of union, my Father, to which I seek to bring all people. For without thee at the center of life, not as a theory but as an experience, life is only one-tenth lived. It is the emanation of your love that gives us rebirth, that gives us hope. And it is manifested in multiple ways, if we but have eyes to see.

Touch each one here today; bring to them thy healing love. We love thee, Father. Thou art our Father and our Mother. And you love us more than we could ever love thee. Thank you, Father. Thank you, Mother. All of these things I pray in thy holy name.

Now, God is here, present in each of you today. It is he who brought us together. Allow yourself for a moment to give thanks that you could be called into a circle of love like this, when you are surrounded by so many, right next door, across the street, down the street—all over this area of the city and beyond—who will not have this great privilege of meeting Spirit face-to-face while still on earth.

You have heard clearly the words of Mr. Baronowski [quoted in the Preface, Part I of this book]. He is here now in the room today [he passed over in 2002], and he supplies part of my laughter, for he was a man of great humor. The witness that he gave to Philip was genuine. And only if you were cynical or a doubting Thomas could you ever question if there was a great element of Spirit here operating. Such missions as this could not have this kind of longevity without authenticity.

Listening to the Inner Voice

I made my entrance into human flesh a long time ago. But I have come back in a most specific way, through this sensitive man whose instrumentality I am using. And it is with great joy that I have found him not to be wanting when it comes to obeying. This is an example for you to follow, meaning, obey the inner voice. Learn to hear it specifically, personally, for you. Granted, it may be out of harmony with what other people think you should do, even those who live with you, right next to you. God will never put you at variance with someone simply for that purpose, but may allow you to test your faith—to follow or not follow the inner voice.

Many times this person I am using was at variance with his family. His children did not particularly enjoy his gift as they grew older. They are somewhat in distance to it, meaning the world has their attention. Love and marriage and children have their attention, as it should be. And so there are many times when I called him, when he alone understood the call, and answered, and obeyed.

There have been those who have gone away from his work, who are now coming back to it. They made their venture out into the world away from this work, to find that they were hungry again for it. And more and more this shall happen. It is not he who is doing the work. He is the vessel we are using. But if it were not for his cooperation and his ongoing prayer and meditation life, the quality of this work could not be as it is. I could not be sustained for this great length of time to speak to you if he was average. Rare is such an opportunity!

Why do I speak this way? It is not to make him look or feel special, rather so that you will understand your own value; that you will cooperate with Spirit, and allow yourself to be used in whatever way you are called to be used.

Going to God. . .Within

When we talk about going within and meeting God within, I want you to think with me as to your motive for such an effort. It is one thing to go to God because you need something. Many people do that. And that is okay. He gave you life; he is your eternal parent, the Parent of us all. And so you have that right to ask and have your needs fulfilled.

But the child who is most valuable to the parent, the one to whom the parent is most attracted is the one who says, "Father, Mother, you've already worked very hard for me. You don't need to worry about my needs. They are given to me plentifully through divine law. You have provided for me up to this point. I have never wanted for anything, not truly. But I want to come here to be with you, just to be with you. I want to hold your hand, as you hold mine. I want to bask in your love and have you feel my love. I just want to be here, to be here for you." In that kind of love, dear ones, God will respond so quickly.

So when you go into your meditations, do not treat God as some distant being whom you have to meet in time. He is in you, now. He wants to appear to you *now*. He wants to envelope you *now*. And he wants to experience you in him *now*.

You do not have to go to God as a beggar. God, like the sun, is ever giving. You only have to hold your hands out to receive what he has to give. The sun is ever shining in spite of earthy circumstances or the circumstances of your life. God, our Father and Mother, is always giving; always giving.

At one time through these lips, I said that God is not a stingy God. Just the opposite. He is the source of all life, because he is the source of all love. And love, by its very intrinsic nature, wants to give out. It also wants to receive, but it wants to give out even more! And so God is ever giving—giving, giving, giving, giving. There is no time in which God is somehow holding back.

Relating to God

The idea in your religious teachings that you have to placate God, or you have to cause God to somehow favor you is in great error. God already favors you; he gave you life! There's no need to win his favor. He loves you under all circumstances. He takes care of you under all circumstances. There is no time in which God ever removes himself from you. But he, forever and forever and forever and forever, finds his dwelling place in you personally. *Personally.* And so there is no need to beg God.

Rather than tell him what you need, say this: "Father, you know what I need. I am just here waiting to receive it." Whatever your venture is now, whatever you are trying to do with your life, it's much easier for God to give to you when you're standing tall to receive, rather than on begging knees. And hold your arms out and say, "Father, I am ready. Please give me what you're ready to give." And rather than pronouncing what he should give to you, let him give what he knows you need.

There are wants and there are needs. Again, let him give to you what you *need.* Many are the things we think we need; we do not. Many a thing that we want, yet once gotten, we find we do not want or need. A bigger house does not make one happier. More money does not make one happier. There are many people with big houses and lots of money. There are people with fame. None of these makes one happier. Deviated human nature is to want more and more and more. Such desire is to our own detriment.

There is only one true desire, one authentic desire that fulfills a need that is ever, ever, ever lasting: the need for God. Jesus indicated this, saying, "Seek ye first the Kingdom of Heaven, and all things shall be added to you." If you're worried about your life, if somehow you are protecting your interests, whatever they may be, fret not. God is protecting you. But you should seek for what he knows you need, rather than what you want. Because in the end, that's what happens anyway. It just means your time climbing up the Mountain of Life takes longer. Because if you would stand with open arms and open hearts, and not try to dictate, but just receive, those things would come flooding to you faster. It's all there. God has before him, so to speak, the buttons that he can push to obtain anything for you. Anything! He can arrange any circumstance, have any spiritual being come, bring money, or do anything.

God Relating to You

While the Israelites, fleeing from Egypt, were crossing the desert wilderness heading toward the Promised Land, God heard their cry for food and miraculously provided them with sustenance in the form of manna. So childlike was their faith and so great was their need, God took it upon himself to feed them.

The Master Jesus had a few fish and bread in a basket, which were multiplied through the intercessory power of God and the spirit world. And with a few loaves of bread and some fish Jesus fed the vast number of people. It is true. It happened.

So examine yourself in this process we're going through—that part of your meditation where we say to go inside and long for God—just long! Just want his presence. And watch how your meditations, your prayer life, your whole life, become accelerated.

These are my words to you today. I deeply appreciate your participation, making it possible for me to have an audience that is cooperative, that is interested, that is inspired and inspires me.

God bless you. This is Saint Germain.

Ever Follow
The Guiding Star

THIS IS SAINT GERMAIN. GOD BLESS YOU.

I have stepped through Philip that I may come directly to you and lend not only knowledge but also my love.

I have surrounded you in this moment with my Violet Light, and this light emanates to your husband, as well.

In the Eye of the Hurricane

You, dear one, have studied for years the theory that when two people center upon God that experience will cause them or enable them to become one in him. That, indeed, is a fact, but the reality that you human beings must work through is such that the ideal, the perfect, cannot be realized quickly. For in your generation the effort toward this precious ideal of oneness with God at this level has seldom, if ever, been reached. You are pulling the weight of history behind you. I am not telling you anything new. But because you are each more than the sum total of yourselves, then the encumbrances of the past, personal and ancestral, weigh heavily upon your ability to go forward. Therefore, the ideal cannot be quickly or readily reached. Nevertheless, as with a voyager upon a stormy sea, if he loses sight of the guiding star, meaning the divine ideal, certainly his journey will be in vain and he will be lost at sea.

It still stands true that God, in all of his manifestations outside of you and inside of you, is still the Star to follow. The degree of effort and faith toward that goal, individually and collectively, tells you in the equation what kind of success that equals. This does not mean that you do not have to deal with personal, inner problems. But ultimately the solution to human conflict and problems does not lie in focusing upon the conflict or the problem. Nor does resolution come through holding grudges or maintaining negative thoughts or feelings.

The conscious inclusion of God in one's life is the means to the changing of the human soul and returning to that reality called God. When you are in a hurricane, you can be hit by many flying objects, you can be whirled about, tossed about, or even killed. But if you will run into the eye of the hurricane—in this case, God—there you will regain a center of calm.

Transforming Your Energies

The true simple secret to success in marriage, all things being equal, is to realize that God is in you, and in each other. Literally talk about it with one another, and talk about what it means to treat each other as God.

Each time there is anger, each time there is accusation, each time there is the exchange of negative words, you are not only responsible for hurting each other, but you are hurting God within. Does this mean that we should not argue? Does this mean that we should not be in conflict? Does this mean that we should not ferret out the truth of things? No. But do it in the context of prayer, much prayer. If you cannot agree upon prayer, do it then in congenial conversation.

Most people that I seek to help through this channel do not approach their life through logical means. Their responses are emotional and visceral. It is best to use the combination of human intelligence and the human heart to discern things.

Whenever you find yourselves in this kind of difficulty where you are unable to come into agreement, you must both call a truce. You must *re-channel* that energy which you would give out in negative form. You must stop and think before you speak, and thoughtfully, purposely transform your anger, frustration and hurt.

When these things cycle and recycle through our being, they only keep negative energies alive. The creative process which God has given to you is the ability to stop, to look, to listen, to observe your own thoughts, and to pick and choose that thought you will express to each other in the most positive terms, with no barbs of hate or anger.

You must consciously take those atoms in the matrix of negative energy and, through willpower, transform them to positive energy. This does not mean that pain would completely dissipate. But you must understand the law of life: whatever you give out, you will eventually get back.

Therefore, when two are in conflict, one of the two has to be big enough to forgive. Someone must stop the onslaught and the circulation of negative to indifferent energies from passing back and forth.

The Secret of the Saint

At this very moment Jesus is very near you. The reason is multiple, but it is he who took his love, who took his energies and gave the example of how to transform one's life—even under the most destructive circumstances as in his crucifixion—into something higher and filled with goodness.

The difference between saint and non-saint is not the difference in the content of one's life. The difference is in how one *handles* life. To the spiritually elevated person, every struggle spells opportunity. Instead of denying or running away from their struggles, the saint faces them boldly with a humble attitude in an effort to learn what suffering has to teach them.

Dear ones, none of what I have said to you is new. None of it is new or something you have not thought about in some way. But I am lending my energies—as a force behind your couple—through these words and there will be a residue of my energies left with you both. Work with them. Contemplate my words. Think deeply upon them, for it is in the grasping of this reality—of learning to transform energy—that we truly achieve self-mastery.

Life was meant to be lived orderly and constructively, not randomly and negatively. And it was meant to be lived objectively, meaning it was meant to be lived so that it might conform to God's will. All of this is necessary for the human being to become truly human and one with his higher self and God.

As you listen to my words, as you play my words over—even write them out—you will understand that they ring true and that in their conglomerate reality is a great kernel of truth, a diamond of truth. Apply them and you will find yourself coming to a whole new level of self-realization.

I am going to depart while leaving the fragrance of my holy love with you, holy because I was sent by the Father to do his holy will.

God bless you. This is Saint Germain.

DISCOURSE SEVEN

God's Game of Life

[Prior to Saint Germain's entrance into this channeling session all sat in silent meditation listening to the song *Holy Ground*.

"You're standing on holy ground.

And the Lord is present and where he is, is holy..."]

AM HERE. THIS IS SAINT GERMAIN.

I am so pleased to be back with you. And I feel your welcome. I am also aware of how deeply touched some of you are by this atmosphere. It is ringed [in spirit] with so many people who love you. They are standing all around. And some of you have been very touched, and could feel the vibration of love as they came through, could you not? [Yes.] They are your ancestors. They are those who were especially close to you when they lived on the earth plane. They are also your master teachers and guides who are working so closely with you to make your life more prosperous spiritually, and more joyful than their life was. They are always there and only a thought away.

Indeed, because of your faith, this is honored space. This is hallowed and holy ground. Not only by the energy you have brought here today, but also because of the many meetings you have held in this space. You have built up a vibration, an energy, that we can use to your advantage and ours.

This afternoon will be characterized by a different kind of feeling, because we have overshadowed you with a different kind of energy. We will continue to have our laughter and our joy and our serious talks; also we'll have changes in mood which you have brought with you after eating, but also *we* have brought purposely to create a new environment.

The Perspectives of God

I heard you speaking about the war in Iraq during your lunchtime. There are opinions, many opinions. There are reports and partial reports. Everyone has his or her view. But there truly is only one proper view regarding anything happening on earth, war or otherwise, and that is God's point of view.

The newspaper reporters and television reporters may ask what the soldiers think, what the man on the street thinks, but does anyone ask God what *he* thinks? This is the greatest crime in humanity.

From God's perspective, this war is his experience. *He* is playing the game of war within his own thoughts and mind. This is his dream. But as long as you stand anywhere but at the top of the Mountain—that is, unless you stand one with

God—you're going to get an incorrect perspective. Only at the top can you see all things as they should be seen.

The war that is most serious is the war within the human mind, the conflict between what is good and what is not good, to do this, or to do that. But when you have ventured to the top of the Mountain, you see it all from a completely different perspective. There is no good or bad: no one is born and no one dies. Each person who is on the battlefield today is not there by accident. Even when they made their choice to sign on the dotted line, to join their particular branch of service, to be a soldier, they were animated by the intelligence of God to play out their role, their script. Not one of them is there by some capricious decision on God's part.

God is simply projecting himself out from the field of light that he is—through a matrix of energy—which is registered within his own consciousness. By clicking on an icon on your computer screen you may access a library of information. The icon which you click to access the Internet is a tiny, simple thing which is a golden doorway into worlds upon worlds of information.

An icon is but a representation and not the thing that it represents itself. A picture of Jesus, as an icon, is not the man Jesus. The man Jesus is much more than the sum total of his picture. And so it is with each human being. We are but a small representation of the God and Creator behind our existence. We are, in fact, projections of God, himself, into a smaller and representative form, that when we open up to the reality of ourselves within, each of us can find the very presence of God! Perhaps now you can understand what I mean when I say, "All is God and no one is born and no one dies!"

I do not mean to make light of what appears to be suffering. Or for the bloodshed that appears within this dream. But for you who are being ushered along the path toward the *top* of the Mountain, it becomes you to look at all of this correctly.

The individual who harbors anger toward another is only fooling himself. Since all is one, there is no other who is against you. In fact, since all is one, the appearance of "another" is illusionary.

Of course, because it is God playing this role, it will be played to the hilt, even in the roles in which there appears to be indifference to life or laziness. It is how people, playing their roles, are programmed.

Ever Expanding Eternal Spirit

God took on this body called "you," that through the interaction between your spirit and your body, you could grow. Grow what? Grow and pass through the grades of spiritual understanding. That is why he created the physical body and designed this interaction between the two, that both may benefit, that it may be a win-win situation.

The body serves the spirit as the host. And the two interact in their energy at all times but most especially and intensely through the use of the science called "meditation." As understanding dawns within the human mind at higher and higher levels, you then can see life increasingly from your original self: "I am God, I am not different from God. I see that I have created a world in which I am having the pleasure, the enjoyment, of knowing who I am. I have created all kinds of situations with all kinds of complexities, all kinds of characters, that I might know myself from every angle, to discover every facet of who I am. To expand my knowledge, expand my joy, my pleasure."

There is no blood spilled in a dream. When you wake up in the morning and you have dreamt that you cut yourself or you were at war, you can look all over your bed sheets and you will not find a drop of blood. Why? Because the dream has taken place in your mind. All of this is taking place in the theater of God's mind. The tanks, the gunshots, the blue sky, the birds singing. The trees blowing in the wind. You. All of life.

So you came to the earth plane as God taking on the shell of a body for the interaction between the two, that through life in general, and meditation specifically, you would awaken from the illusion. As God, you purposely drew a veil over the mysteries of life, over your own consciousness, that you could have the pleasure of playing, pretending and enjoying the drama of it all.

As I have said before, it is all like a child who plays with little metal soldiers and tanks. If, with a boyfriend he is doing this in earnest, he may forget that he's just playing games, and even get angry at his playmate. So much so as to even throw something at him or yell at him, or become upset. You have seen children doing this many times. It is an illusion. There is no war. No one is hurt. There is no enemy. It is all one energy. Pretend, pretend, pretend. Make believe, make believe. But during that time, the child has drawn a veil over his own mind of "forgetfulness." At any moment he can awaken to the fact that, "Hey, this isn't really a war. These are just little metal things I'm pushing around on the rug.

And Tommy's not my enemy—what am I doing here?" But instead, he enjoys the game and forgets. Where does this nature come from? Who created this kind of scenario which is found everywhere on earth? It is God.

There are people communicating, people fighting, people laughing, people making love, people having babies, people eating, people sleeping, people climbing mountains, people going into valleys, people cutting down trees, people planting trees. It is raining here and sun shining there; and thunder and lightening, floods, earthquakes, sunshine, spring, winter, happen all over the globe—all at the same time. All kinds of scenarios are being played out on earth. And God is enjoying it all.

Don't forget that you are God. It is why we are teaching you in class each week to say, "I am God, I am not different from God. I am the indivisible, supreme absolute. I am being, awareness, bliss." The "I" in this mantra is referring to you as "I—God," and not your earthly self which I call your "little I." When you say it again and again, remember that you are using the capital "I." I—am not these thoughts. I, God, am not these feelings. I, God, am not this mind; I am not this body. I am—**I AM, I AM, I AM**—ever expanding, eternal spirit. **I AM God!**

Where you are going is away from the illusion to wake up from how others are fearful and paralyzed by what appears to be real. Yes, as long as you are *in* the illusion, you must play your part. Each of you goes to a job or does some kind of work to make money. That's a part of the illusion, but you still go and do it.

Yes, you carry it out because it's a part of your role until you fully awaken. Once you fully wake up, as has happened to some of humanity such as the great masters, you will no longer search anywhere. Most of their day is spent contented in meditation whether at work or play. What they need is brought to them, for they have mastered themselves. They have brought themselves to the apex of the Mountain. They are fully empowered with all the qualities of God himself, for God in that person has awakened, and is able to draw to themselves what they need, by the power of being God.

You do not need to be pulled down by any of what appears on earth. Remain objective, aloof if you will, showing your empathy, your compassion where needed. But do not get caught up in it yourself.

One of the reasons that I and others brought some Iraqi soldiers here was so they could hear me talk about this point. So they do not wander about in the spirit world on the plains of Iraq, carrying a gun, thinking they are still alive. I wanted them to be able to awaken to the reality that it is all an illusion. That they may transcend into the higher planes of the spirit world.

God's dispensation of the world today allows for this more immediate help. They have died for a cause which they did not start. Nor will they end it. They are, in many cases, the innocent victims of other men's vanities and egos. Therefore, they rank high in deserving our love and support.

The Magnificent Reality of Self

HIS IS SAINT GERMAIN. GOD BLESS YOU.

I was, indeed, doing the things which Philip talked about with healing you, and you are making great progress. When you look back on the meager beginnings of your stepping out into the healing work, you have come a long, long way. We have been guiding your every step. You must know and affirm and have complete confidence that you are never alone. You are always surrounded by your guides and your teachers. In those times when you feel very alone, please call upon us for our help.

When you call upon us, you must not call in vain, but you must—in your own faith, from the strength of your own soul—affirm that we have come and are delivering the help you seek. Our ability to help is limited, not by our degree of ability, but more by how much you have faith and trust in our ability to help you.

The child-like mental stance is that vibration which enables us most fully to enter into your activities to help bring about the desired changes and the meeting of your needs.

The timing of this [spiritual] reading is perfect. We do not want you to falter. We do not want you to step back. When the soul loses faith and belief in itself, it is the worst kind of situation. It is good to observe yourself as to the rightness or wrongness of anything that you do. In this way we each guide ourselves to correct ends. But any manner of self-condemnation is totally inappropriate. We do not condemn, so why should you condemn—either yourself or someone else?

God is the Eternal and the Infinite

We can never go forward and backward at the same time without either being confused or torn apart. As we observe ourselves—maintaining maximum objectivity—we can monitor where we are going and make corrections as needed.

It is a waste of energy to be negative. That same energy should be used to gain understanding and correct our course. Those who have learned to center completely upon God, lead their life in this way and become successful, if not in the worldly sense, then in the spiritual sense.

It is because God is the Source of all life that his attitude toward himself is always positive. He knows who he is 100% of the time. He has no doubt about who he is or where he is going. And it is by the means just described that he guides himself to the right ends. He, being the center and creator of all that is, cannot afford to do less as he keeps himself ever moving forward and upward, never backward and downward. In this state of mind, God is ever renewed—as he never becomes tired and never grows old! Those who find and follow him within the domain of themselves will only prosper as he prospers.

During those times when you go into meditation and don't feel anything or cannot center, do not wrestle with it. Rather, accept that it is a phase. During that time, gaze into yourself and ask the paramount question, "Who am I?" You will be made very clearly aware, in time and through this kind of inquiry, that you are not the body or its many needs. You shall be permanently grounded in the realization that you are limitless love and life. You are God.

As I have said, each human being is an emanation from the mind of God. Out of his reflecting and pondering, out of his loving and caring, you came to be. He gave birth to you as a soul by projecting your image, through sound and inner visualization, into existence. It was his love for the ideal you—a reflection of his own image—that willed him to bring you into reality.

It is the on-going circuitry of his love that flows through you always. God is eternal and infinite. These two aspects are part of his nature. This is what gives you and me our eternal and infinite nature.

In this critical time, as I said, we do not want you to falter or fall back. Because of this, it is important to revisit that magnificent reality of self within. By continuing to realize who you really are—God in you, you in God—you have all that you need to go forth and be all you are intended to be.

It is not by your volition alone, for the more that you humble yourself to the reality of which I speak—God in man, man in God—and become a channel, the more will you come to be your real self, and the more successful will your life become.

It is by focusing upon this internal vibration, which to many is heard as an *aum* sound, or the God presence within you, that you will have all that you need, and give birth to an ever-expanding being.

Live up to your noblest ideals. Live up to your purest thoughts, and follow the wisdom which you have been given. You will pass through this period very quickly. We have willed it so. As you detach yourself from ego to attach yourself to the larger sphere of God's heart—and you will learn more and more how to do that—the easier will it be for you to put past things past and move forward.

Doing Unto Self

As Philip said, there are great things planned for you. "Great things" does not mean fame and fortune, it means opportunities for spiritual growth and for the reaching out in service to a large body of humanity. It is in the dynamic of reaching out to others that we will be reaching out to you, and the self-realization you are seeking will come most fully.

You have come to understand that it is not enough to give lip service to faith. It is not enough simply to reach out to heal others, but you must be about the business of also reaching out to *you*. You have been taught that the healer really cannot heal adequately unless he or she is healed. A balance must be struck, of course, of reaching into self and out to others.

Don't forget to give to yourself the healing love that you would give others. Don't forget to forgive yourself of your human frailties as you would help others to forgive theirs. Do unto self in love as you would do unto others. Then this time will quickly pass.

Love, which emanates from God, is the love that you will be seeking ultimately in yourself and in the one whom you will ultimately find as your life partner. It is, as always, my great joy and pleasure to serve you in this way and to be a part of the small and large steps you take toward the advent of your own spiritual perfection. That is, indeed, what this life's earthly journey is truly all about.

Go forth. First go in faith, and from that will flow to you and through you all the other understanding that you need. It is there waiting before you, waiting for you to reach out and receive it.

God bless you. This is Saint Germain.

DISCOURSE NINE

Weaving God's Tapestry

AM HERE. THIS IS SAINT GERMAIN.

I am so very, very pleased to be able to make this entrance into your world. I recognize faces here who have prayed for this work. It is all one work. All that is happening at any time on your earth is a part of the grand plan. And because you are caught in the time warp of your existence, you see it in a very different way from how *we* see it. For if you could see human history and the history of the universe, from its creation until now, you would have a much better perspective of the reality in which you are existing. I, Saint Germain, and those of us who come for this great work that you are doing, have this vantage point.

Why we want to come and support all that you are doing for the good of mankind is because we know the bigger picture. The thread of your work—your individual work—must be woven into the tapestry of the entire work, that it all may be completed in God's time.

77

Beloved ones, the work that you do is a thread attached to those who will follow you, as it is a thread attached to those have gone before you. Together, those of you who are here now, those who have gone before you now in spirit, and those who are not even yet born who will pick up this work, are part of the weaving of a massive, massive tapestry.

It is a glorious creation—so very beautiful and so meaningful to the One who gave life to all. When you are a single thread or a thread-bearer, you cannot see the whole tapestry. Therefore, you cannot see the value of your individual threads. Be assured that you are, at all times, being woven into the eternal tapestry of life. And if you will listen to the interior of yourself, that holy place Philip spoke about in the beginning of this evening, you will get that confirmation that you are in the right place at the right time.

Never mind your critics. What is most important is what *God* thinks, for he is the final determiner of what shall be done with your work. No human being can have the all-encompassing, timeless vision God has. It is he who has been orchestrating all of life, and he has used every avenue, every channel, every opportunity, every individual, every word and every prayer, every note in every song that was ever sung of his glory. He has used all of this and more to draw mankind to himself.

When you can see that and when you can comprehend that he is so all-encompassing, that he loves the so-called "heathen" as much as he loves the so-called "devout," you are on your way to truly knowing God.

While he can see each of you from an exterior point of view, he is infinitely more interested in seeing your heart. In this way he knows you from the inside out. And not only does he know your potential for this life, but for eternity. The Parent of us all sees each of us as himself, for he took from himself to create all of us!

We are all mirrors to him. It is all his energy. The very fabric of your being, both physical and spiritual, consists of the atoms, the light energy that came from God almighty! It is through this realization that you come to know that all is one.

The Search for Truth

The hunger, the longing, the quest—that unquenchable thirst to know the very truth of things—did not come from you. It is the message sown in your own soul. It leads you on saying, "I need more! I need to search further and higher. I need the answers to more questions." Who planted within you the unabated desire to know higher and higher truth? It was not you. It was God.

You were born with this desire, even as you were born with the desire for food. But that food which your soul desires is truth. What food is to the body, truth is to the mind, to the soul. From the time you took your first breath, you began questing to know your real self—that *being* in whom God is infused totally and completely.

Jesus, the Christ, is not different from you in your potential. It is just that he was aware from a very young age and left no stone unturned in the search for truth. His time away from the world was spent looking for the truth. He advanced quickly because he was in earnest. He was gifted spiritually from birth and greatly perfected and magnified these gifts by far above average dedication to his quest for God and to know his real self. Through his spiritual openness he could communicate interiorly and directly with God.

It was this experience that led him to know that he and all of us are temples of God. He ardently proclaimed this truth to all who would listen.

Because Jesus was so filled with the presence of God, he proclaimed that in seeing him [Jesus] one could see the Father and that he and the Father were one. He laid no *exclusive* claim to this fact but let us know that we, too, are the temples of God. And I, Saint Germain, proclaim and maintain, as Jesus did, that God is immanent in all human beings!

Connecting to the Heart of God

You have two hearts. You have the physical heart which you can feel beating in your body this moment, but if you could see with spiritual eyes, you would realize it is beating because right next to it—in spirit—is your spiritual heart, which sends its electrical impulse through the electric body into the nervous system to the brain and into the heart. But what is the energy behind the heartbeat of the spiritual heart? That heart is connected to the very heart of God.

Did you ever think that each time your heart beats it is the beat of God's heart *in* your heart causing it to do so? Because God is beyond time and space, then there is a stream of energy that runs to each individual. As it does, he has contact with each of you and he exists in you. He is *in* you, and yet he is outside of you and all around you. You are like a proverbial fish in water; the water is in you and all around you. God is totally in you, and totally around you.

To fulfill the purpose of this life and realize your divine destiny, you need to realize fully, through direct experience, the reality of God in you and you in God. It is through progressive understanding and experiences that we advance ever closer to him.

Our Father works through all levels of religious teachings and revelations (ours and others') as means to reaching him. God, the author of all truth, will never change. But to get to him we must deepen and expand our understanding. This is imperative.

The child within the womb could not stay there much beyond nine months. It is an impossible environment in which to be contained forever. And so, the "womb" of your understanding, at any one time, is there to give you birth into a greater understanding. If it were not so, what value would eternity have, if it is simply to do the same thing again and again? If it is simply to reinvent the wheel? To cover the same roads and pathways, it would indeed, be a very, very meaningless eternity. But life is an adventure, traversed by *ever-increased* understanding. The great ones among you are those who have dared to go beyond and find higher and higher truth.

I did not say to throw things out in your quest. Stand with the truth that still has meaning to you. In the first grade you learned the alphabet and how to read simple words. None of that experience was negated as you moved up into higher grades. Looking back on your educational beginnings, you can see what you learned was the truth but that there was subject matter far beyond the mere alphabet and greater work than learning to read three and four letter words.

It is the nature of truth to be comprehended according to our level of understanding. As our understanding increases and expands, so does our comprehension of the truth of things. Be ever ready to answer the quest calling from within, and dare to question. And in questioning, you will inevitably be led to higher and higher truth.

This process, dear friends, is an eternal one. You will never, ever, ever come to the end of knowing yourself, even as you will never come to knowing God completely.

How boring a relationship would be between husband and wife if they did not discover new facets of one another. If there was not something to explore beyond the initial romance and the struggles. All of life is ever, ever evolving, ever becoming greater than it is, ever going beyond its parameters to a higher existence, into a higher dimension. This is because you and I come from a God of limitless love, limitless understanding, and limitless expansion of both.

Learning the Lessons

You are here now, whether you understand my words or not. This very moment as you hear these words—being where you are in your spiritual search and understanding—you are exactly where you are because God put you here. Ask that question which Philip posed in the beginning: "What is it that I am to learn on this rung of the ladder? What is it that I am to gain from this experience?" The essential question is: *Who am I?* As you gradually answer that question, its answer will take you into higher and higher levels of understanding, spiritual experiences and definitely closer and closer to God.

To overcome the vicissitudes of this life, the extremities, the sufferings, the valleys, the dark times, you need not fight them. All you need to do is turn to the light within yourself. And you do this by the inquiry into self that I have just mentioned.

I, Saint Germain, am able to channel through to you in this way, because as a being of light I synchronize the frequency of my light force with that of Philip Burley's. More specifically, I am speaking to you as a spiritual being whose essence is also light. This is the light I speak of when I speak of synchronizing my light frequency with Philip's.

This light essence, call it soul, call it *atma,* call it spirit; whatever name you may call it, matters not. This light that you are is unchanged and unaffected by anything, for it is the light of God manifesting as your eternal self. Therefore, when you go within and turn to this illumination that you are, you are turning to an unwavering, unchanging light of love and truth. It is your resting place of ultra-stability and understanding.

See Yourself

Beloved ones, you *are* light beings! If you could but see your own light—and you *need* to see your own light—it would be possible for you to view your own spiritual being. Only ignorance and lack of life experience has kept you from it. But if at this very moment I could open your spiritual eyes, allowing you to see the very reality of yourself, you would stand in absolute awe of the beauty of your soul!

Again, to drive home the point loudly and clearly: that light can never be shut out, can never go away, can never be removed, for it is that spark which God gave to you from the beginning which is the *real* you. The "higher self," you call it. It is not a stranger to you. It is that part of you that sends forth ideas of virtue, lofty dreams and visions. It is the super-conscious part of your mind.

When your body is dirty, you don't look at the dirt and say, "Oh, I am dirty." Rather, you know underneath that dirt is a clean body. You don't focus upon the dirty water of the bath. You wash off the dirt, and when you step from your bath you are clean. So it is with the human being. However anyone may argue this point, the pure fact is, you are already made of light. It is only the layers of ignorance and the misuse of life's energies which have created this barrier, this undesirable dirt—if you will—in your life.

But you need not dwell upon the exterior realities of your life, any more than you need to dwell upon the dirt on your body or the dirty bath water. Let it go down the drain of forgetfulness; let it swirl away. Let God take care of it. The past is past. We are existing *now*, and the sooner you awaken to this light within you, the sooner you will come to view it and celebrate your glory.

When I say "glory," I do not use this word in an earthly sense. That is not what the light body is made of. Meaning, it is not prideful or in need of praise or adulation. It is made of pure love, unselfish love. Unselfish love is your essence, for it is the essence of God. How else could he create all of this to share the abundance, the infinite variety and beauty? All was given for you. The essence of yourself is unselfish. In those moments of reverie you know that. It is only your fear of loss, due to attachment, which keeps you from giving out more freely.

Allowing Your Light to Shine

Give out! Let that natural self shine through the portals of your present existence! Ninety percent of the world's problems would be over *overnight*, if everyone would learn to center on others and forget self. It is that light within you that needs to shine into this world. It is that light within you that becomes the rays for the channeling of all goodness, and that shines forth when you give out.

I do not mean that you should not take care of this light. You need that private time. You need that time to become familiar with yourself. A large percentage of your meditation should be spent in self familiarization—getting to know the *real* you. For you do not know the real you yet. If you did, you would not struggle. The conflicts, the difficulties, the worries would cease and you would exist in that perpetual state which God, our Father and Mother, exists in—perpetual peace. It is an immovable, unchangeable peace.

Fear Not the Future

Oh how much, how very much I want to share with you all that I know. Instead of pouring a few cupfuls of this truth that is known in my place of existence, I want so ardently to pour an unending waterfall of truth to quicken your awareness.

Let me say this: you are all on such good paths. Fear not the future. You are all being guided by divine intervention. There is no time in which you are alone or out of the thought of God. You are a part of God's very existence as much and more than your hand is a part of your body. It is an extension of you. There is no way you could forget it! How much more is this true of the relationship between a parent and her child? You are *why* our Heavenly Father exists. He loves you as much as he loves himself. Trust him in all things.

Life is Eternal, Cyclic, & Growing

I AM HERE. THIS IS SAINT GERMAIN.

I wish you the most joyful and prosperous New Year. I have been away for a while; not away from my medium, but away from you, the listening audience. I am sure you have missed hearing from me, as many of you have written and called, and said you enjoy this part of the work that we do together here on the radio. I am always so pleased that I can have this opportunity to use this instrument, and to use the medium of radio to reach many thousands of people. It is a benefit of this age that I did not have in former ages. And I am exceedingly grateful to Providence who has made it possible for us to come through.

[Saint Germain led a meditation in which each of the colors of the chakras was mentioned.]

Now, dear friends, know this: as you meditate and focus on each individual color of your chakras, like the colors of the rainbow in the sky, these are the monumental steps of life—as you ascend the Mountain of Self—which my medium has come to call the Golden Path. Herein lies the true course, the ultimate path for self-purification and development.

As you climb higher and higher on a mountain, the view changes and the air is more rarified. So, too, on the spiritual mountain, as you ascend to its summit; the view changes as you gain more elevated understanding and attain uncommon spiritual development by which you obtain a whole new perspective of self, of life, and of God. At this spiritual elevation you have reached the seventh chakra and above, at which time full divinity can manifest and self-mastery will have been achieved.

When you come into this higher level of self, particularly through the chakras of heart, throat, third eye, and crown, you will awaken to the gifts of the Spirit and can, at will, perform miracles, perceive of the afterlife, and be a channel as my medium is, if you are so inclined. But most important is what this level of spiritual achievement can do for helping yourself. That is what it is all about: personal perception, personal intuition, personal awakening.

And in the center of all is the great light of God's presence, which never removes itself. That is the light of your life, without which you would have no life or existence. For it is that Center who coalesced you into the being you are now, both in your physical body and in your spirit. Know this. *Live* this.

Living Life

Life is eternal. And life is to be lived as if it is eternal. Too often, we identify only with the physical body. In a world of growing materialism and great emphasis upon the physicality of existence, there is the fading of awareness of who we really are. You are not this physical body. And when you look into the mirror each day, if you but had spiritual sight, you could see that beyond this physical body is your spiritual self. It is the real you, the center of consciousness. It is that part of you which perceives higher vibrations, which partakes of the spiritual world now.

You stand between two worlds, the spiritual and the physical. And even as thought is invisible yet real—powerful, potent—so your spiritual being, while invisible, indiscernible to you through physical awareness, is very real—palpable, eternal. It is the center of your real self. When you sleep at night this part of you can rise from the physical body to partake of the pranic force surrounding it, breathing it in, bathing in this energy. It may go off into various realms of the spiritual world to visit, learn, and be educated. At an appointed time your spirit self then comes back, through the vortex of the physical energy, to resume life again in the physical body upon awakening.

Life, being eternal, must be thought of and examined from an eternal perspective. If, in fact, you think that there is only physical life and fail to examine your life from an eternal point of view, you will be hard pressed when you come to my side of the universe [the spiritual world] to adjust fully and completely. And you will be drawn back to your attachments on the earth plane. In doing so, you could easily become entrapped in those remembrances and attractions.

It is okay to take care of your physical body; indeed, it is vitally important. It is okay to accumulate material goods; you need them to a certain point. And it is rightful to enjoy that which you eat, preparing things that are tasty and attractive, that you dress in clothes you like to wear and can afford. I am not speaking about these attractions. I am merely saying that when your physical body takes precedence over a growing awareness and awakening of your spiritual self, then you trap yourself in vibrations that you may regret in the future.

For there are—as I have said many times, and it is something you all know—no exceptions to death. All of you who are listening will one day leave your physical body. If you do not hear me consciously now, the words that I speak to you will reverberate in your consciousness when you die. And you will remember. You may not remember my name, but you *will* remember that I told you there is life beyond. That it is important to prepare, and at least to have understanding of the reality of life beyond.

The Spiral of Life

Life is cyclic. Just as we are now following the manmade calendar and have crossed a certain point we call a new year, we are going through a new cycle of 365 days. You have the opportunity to revisit things that you could not accomplish last year, particularly projects that have to do with working on your own self, your own growth, your own awakening.

But, dear friends, life is more than cyclic; life is an ever-ascending spiral. You're not meant to go again and again, around and around in a circle, making the same errors day after day, year after year. I daresay within the sound of my voice, there are many who have things they wish they could undo, or wish they could rid their lives of. Again and again I speak of finding the things that hold them down and keep them from going forward into the higher levels of the spiral. If you want to speak of eternity or the model of life, it is the spiral which approximates most exactly the journey of life.

As I brought you through the meditation, going from point to point, level to level within self awareness—from the lower chakra which represents earthly attachments and aware-ness, to the highest level, the crown chakra, which represents spiritual attainment, and self mastery—this was done through a spiral effect.

You're not meant to be just attached to the physical world. There is more to life than just appetites for the physical. There are the appetites of the soul, that long for and need to be fed with higher and higher understanding. When you were a child, it was okay to study arithmetic. But as you got into the higher levels of your intellectual growth and understanding, you came to study higher math, and would find it, though under-standable, less meaningful, too, to solve simple problems in arithmetic than to work with algebra or geometry, and so on. In your spiritual life you are meant to cycle, to spiral higher and higher in understanding.

The Essence of You

You see, growth is the purpose of life—growth through love. First of all, grow to love yourself by understanding yourself. Many of you do not like yourself. That's because you do not understand yourself. If you could see yourself as I do—as master teachers and more spiritually developed individuals see you—you would see yourself as a divine being—not only filled with light, but you would see that your whole essential, eternal being is made of light *itself*. You would come to comprehend that you have an eternal reality. That you shall never die. That you have powers far, far beyond what you discern.

Some of you are amused by my manifestation here, perhaps believing it is a good form of acting. Indeed, I am acting, but it is not a performance. It is the mastering of these energies as has been done in part by my medium and myself, individually and cooperatively, that makes this manifestation possible.

Those of you who truly perceive of its magnificent reality—not the personalities, but the phenomena—will stand in awe of this possibility. Would we come through to all of you in a similar way, through your own energies? We do, in part, but not to the full extent that is possible. Beyond mediumship, beyond healing, beyond all of this, is the opportunity to leave your physical body at night to explore the spirit world and gain the knowledge of our existence and come back with that knowledge consciously. That is an art form; it is something, through mastering self, you can achieve in this lifetime. You do not have to wait to die in order to know of us or spend conscious time with us.

Growth from where to where? Growth from ignorance to enlightenment. Growth from attachment to the earthly to attachment to the heavenly. In the millions of years that man has existed, has he grown? Have we gone far from the days of the cave man to where we are today? Yes, in many ways we have. As the many calendars of life have passed, man has acquired deeper and higher knowledge. Otherwise, man would be nothing but an animal and would still live in caves and have little understanding of his own psychology or spirituality.

There is plentiful proof of man's evolution over eons of time. Tomes of written information alone are testimony to man's intellectual progress, not to mention endless numbers of inventions and discoveries. Man's comprehension of life, including to a significant degree—how his mind and body function—lend further evidence to just how very, very far man has come in human history. With his genius, man has evolved to a level of great objectivity in the use of his intuitive, spiritual side; having successfully experimented with mind to mind communication, remote viewing, to the control of his body temperature through conscious mind control, to understanding the relationship between the state of the mind and the health of the human body. All of this, and a whole lot more, demonstrate man's great progress on planet earth.

So man *has* evolved; he has grown from where he was to a higher level. But there is still some distance to go beyond that. There are still higher regions of awareness to be obtained. There are still finer experiences to be had. And that's why I am here addressing you in this way: to stimulate within you, as an individual, and collectively as a group, an awareness that you can *in this lifetime*, achieve a high level of spirituality, of spiritual development and awakening, than if you ignore this fact about yourself.

Appreciating Your Journey

Who is responsible for this evolution? This growth from the lower to the higher? From the primitive to the majestic divine?

There are those who would blame others for their suffering. Can you really know that the suffering you go through, you have not attracted to yourself? Can you truly *know* that? Is it true that others have caused you to suffer? Or is it your *response* to adversity that has caused you to suffer?

Those who would curse life because there are undulations—that is today they are high, tomorrow they are low; today they are on the mountain top, tomorrow they are in the valley—are unfortunate. Those who would be upset over life's realities do not understand that this is the rhythm of life. The mountain top and the valley are both there, and all extremes between, to teach us of ourselves. If you embrace both the light and the darkness, and know that both are there for your highest good—by seeking to understand and learn from both—you will grow quickly. When you deny your suffering, that is, when you say life is unfair and unjust, you only lengthen the time you will suffer, or, you will cause yourself to recycle through the same negative experience and not spiral upward.

God is the creator of all. Adversity as well as blessings are both in your life that, through these extremities and all degrees in between, you come to know who you are. For what is life without struggle?

Indeed, those of you who are actively involved in increasing your bodily strength through weight lifting and running and other forms of exercise, understand very clearly that without resistance, without effort—even to the point of muscle-nerve fatigue—the muscles do not grow. The body does not maintain a healthy level without exercise. Indeed, there are those among you who if you would but just get out and walk, even walking only in a shuffle, you would find your health would come back; that by walking *into* the pain, so to speak, for two or three weeks, you would find that the aches and pains would lessen, if not go away.

Because you have married your mind to the thought that as you grow older the decline of your physical body is inevitable, then it *has* become inevitable. It is *you* who locked you into that thought and accepted it as truth, like a religion or belief system, and thus act accordingly, often keeping yourselves in this state of being incapacitated.

You have contracted for this life. Whether you know it or not, you are exactly where you are because you have contracted for it. Pre-existing your birth into human flesh, you existed in consciousness within the mind of God. You pre-existed this entrance with awareness of what life could be on earth, and what price could be paid for what reward. Indeed, you came to this earth to go through the experience, that you might grow in love—love for self, appreciation of your own spiritual powers for life; to learn from whence you came, and to whence you are returning.

Attitude Makes the Difference

You contracted for this life that you may pay off past debts— karmic debts. So those things that appear on your path are there by design. You cannot escape them. And so it is better to say to self, "What is it that I am to learn and to overcome through this experience?" Do not say, "How long must I suffer thusly?" By embracing suffering when it comes, you will shorten that time of suffering, more quickly than if you resist the pain, the difficulty.

After all, it is only your body that dies, that suffers. Not your spirit. Your spirit is made of a fabric that is eternal. It is made of light. It cannot be damaged. Only your thought is in error, and creates the uncomfortable feelings that you experience and the emotional discomforts because of the way you think *about* your suffering. If you would but turn your mind around 180 degrees and embrace your suffering as a blessing, to learn, to grow, to gain freedom from past spiritual debts! *Who knows* the reality of your past life that brought suffering upon you as karma in this life? Perhaps your suffering is due to something you have done to someone in the past, either on earth or perhaps in a past experience or existence. Who can say? I can tell you this is my knowledge and my experience, and pass it on to you, to encourage you under all circumstances to be responsible for your life, and the contract which you have written.

The choice is yours. There is no one who is going to make you do anything. I say this even to those who are suffering and listening to me from prison. Yes, there's a certain routine that you go through daily in prison that may appear monotonous. But it is not that different from the life of a monk who lives in a cloistered situation, who spends time isolated in his cell (as it is called in a convent or monastery) where he prays and meditates sometimes for hours on end. The difference is that the one who renounces his life in the name of religion, has chosen to use his experience, his suffering, the adversity, the loneliness, the isolation, as an opportunity to better his condition, to raise his soul to a higher level of spiritual attainment and awareness.

As you apply an *attitude of gratitude* toward your experience, you will find the prison doors of your heart will open. After all, what can you do in the interim? And is it possible that you contracted for this experience? It is said from our side that fortunate are those who undergo suffering with gratitude, whatever it may be, for they are the ones who will be liberated and find the freedom of this lifetime. The true path, as I have spoken earlier, is the path *inside*.

For of all the religions in the world—which would have you follow a path this way or that—the ultimate reality is that there is only *one* path. And that path is *within* yourself. It is the journey from the external to the internal; from darkness to light; from lower to higher; from grosser to more fine frequencies. Today I described that path in the form of light: the light within you, from the base chakra to the crown chakra. This is the philosophical/spiritual path. It exists literally in the form of light within you. Those who are clairvoyant can see it. And they can interpret its meaning and help adjust it, as you adjusted it today mentally. But it is a real path, a literal path, within you. You ascend it by coming to know the truth of yourself.

Whatever is on your path each day, know that it is being coordinated by the masters of your karma—those who are seeking to help you clear the debit side of your spiritual accounting page to attain a full page of credit. As you acquire understanding, these spiritual truths I speak of, and apply them to your life day after day with gratitude and love, ever observing yourself going through these motions, you will come to understand that you are neither your body, your mind, nor the thoughts that it contains. You are but the observer.

What is at the End of the Path?

You are the individual who is in charge, who never sleeps. Who is it that hears the alarm clock in the morning? If not your physical mind, then it is that which never sleeps within you, the God presence within you, whatever you want to call it—core energy, divine love, unconditional love. It is the core truth, the core reality of yourself, and the journey you make is from the external life to that internal awareness so that heaven may appear to you on earth.

What is the end of the path? It is to realize that you have gone nowhere, and you're returning from nowhere. You're simply awakening by taking off the covers of ignorance resultant from a lack of understanding. You're simply awakening to that which always was. Even as the wave on the ocean may appear momentarily, rising up from the larger body to descend very quickly and be absorbed back into the body of water, it comes from nowhere, it goes nowhere and returns. It comes from the body of water, rising up to fall back again into and be absorbed by that water.

So you, too, dear friends, have risen from God, as waves of expression of himself, in the form of yourself, in a finite way in this physical body. You have taken this form strictly for the experience of amusement, for enjoyment, for learning, for growth. In this way, God has manifested himself in multiple ways, indeed, in *billions* of ways, through the physical body, that in the mirror of you, he may see and know himself. And so what will you discover at the end of this journey? That *you* are that light. That there is only *one* light, and that everything exists within you, because you're the creator of it all. You are God himself.

The path is a path of ascending steps of greater and greater light; brighter and brighter light, until you reach that supreme awareness where everything is light itself. This is the meaning of coming into what we call enlightenment. That's where the word enlightenment comes from. Enlightenment: gaining the light, becoming the light, awakening to the light. You can obtain all of this without having to leave your physical body in what has been called "death."

Marking Your Calendar

As we turn the page to a new 365 days on this manmade calendar, you have the opportunity to utilize the information I have given to you today. I have spoken nothing new. I am only telling you the truth of yourself, reiterated through thousands of thousands of people over millennia.

Those who have awakened to its reality are desirous to help others awaken to it, and understand that the only true religion is the religion of love. That you need to begin with the proper love of self. If you do not love yourself properly, how can you love others? There is that tendency in a religious life to ignore, or put down the physical body, in order to enable the spiritual self to grow—by sacrificing self for others. Sometimes it is taken to such an extreme that at the end of life, such individuals have given everything to everyone except *themselves*. Do not be one of those people.

This year, on your calendar, plan to have personal meetings with yourself. Plan to have conferences with yourself. Plan to evaluate yourself fully, on every level. And listen to yourself. Go into the silence of yourself, into that darkness when your eyes are closed and you're away from the world. There, God speaks. The voice of wisdom is heard. Love issues forth and envelops you.

It is a state of mind which I and many others have achieved, from which one does not want to come back. For in it, you see all things as one. And you know that you're a part of a great body of love, a great wave of love. You know that this body and what you're experiencing is only temporary. And that your goal is far, far reaching; far, far more magnificent; far, far more real than all of life you have experienced up to that point.

That is the promise; that is the hope. That is the journey. And that is the value of taking stock of yourself—of planning your life day by day, week by week, month by month. Take this accounting and examine yourself thoroughly. Being totally honest, not shrinking from the truth, yet not condemning yourself for error.

Both trials and sufferings and periods of calm and peace are a part of God's will for our life. By God's allowing us to have such experiences, we learn and grow and eventually awaken fully to him. What kind of life would it be if one's "land" was only monotonously flat, and there were no mountains or valleys, where everything is the same? It is of no challenge. It is in extremities of experience that the challenge comes, that we grow, and rise up to a whole new level of understanding of ourselves and God.

There are no accidents, dear friends. You are today where you are resultant from all that has gone before. Learn to live now; live right now, *this* day on the calendar. Don't look ahead; don't drag the past behind you. Live now, and live positively. Whatever comes your way, embrace it positively. Bless it, for it to bless you. Embrace it, that it may teach you. Listen to it, that you may grow in understanding from it. And know your own inner power.

This way, and this way alone, will you come to that place Jesus achieved. He knew this. He studied this. He applied this. That's how he knew that he was the living temple of God saying, "He who has seen me has the seen the Father," enabling others to emulate his life. But he was not fully understood; life unfolded still haphazardly, spiritually, religiously. And today we are still seeking to bring that enlightenment, that ultimate truth: that you are the living temple of God; that God exists within you; that the path to personal self-achievement spiritually and eternally is right within your own divine self.

Know that our love follows you and guides you at every turn in the road. You are never alone.

God bless you. This is Saint Germain.

Part Two

Questions & Answers With Saint Germain

Saint Germain, this is John.

Yes, John.

My question has to do with harmonizing one's feelings—meaning with the world being so chaotic, and the anger, irritation, fear and judgment all around us every day—how do we best deal with that chaotic state? How do we stay calm and serene in the midst of it all?

Living in Perpetual Peace

That is a very practical question. Its answer lies in large part in the thing that I described regarding our Creator. There's no way that you can remove yourself from the vibrations of this earth plane. You are in the physical body. And you are conditioned, through childhood and on up in life, to respond to the things as you have been trained to respond. What may be abhorrent to you, to your upbringing, may not be so abhorrent to another who was trained to do a thing that bothers you. Therefore, that conditioning within you is going to make you feel some constraint regarding violence in the world. Or war. Or the idea of the invasion of one country by another country. Or the destruction that might befall your family.

My son, none of this is in your hands. You can move about, you can dig tunnels, you can go to the other side of the earth, but your life is circumscribed, already planned. If you are in harm's way, you cannot stop what may happen to you. All of life, as I spoke of the past, present and the future, is progressing toward higher and higher development. Those who suffer what appears to be injustices on earth are rewarded in the spirit world by higher knowledge, and they are liberated from any presence of resentment or anger or bitterness. Any time something happens that appears to be untoward and unfair here on earth, there is adequate compensation in the spirit world. Why? Because God is just.

Tonight you did a meditation that I oversaw. Partly Philip was inspired by me to provide the content, as I sought to draw closer and closer in preparation to come through him. In this particular meditation we focused upon learning how to find perpetual inner peace. It is not something you have to create. It is something that always is. Learn to go inward by controlling your breath and do the kinds of exercises you are doing, and you will, over time, come to that level, that frequency of peace within yourself and be able to stay there at all times.

This instrument I am speaking through has the ability to maintain a level of calm in the midst of chaos. That did not come simply by birth, though as a soul he came into this life expression as a very calm being essentially. Through training and self-mastery, he has learned to stay in that center of peace within himself, doing the very thing he taught tonight, which is to remain patient above all, and allow the vicissitudes of life to wash over you without disturbing your inner peace. Above all, Philip knows by experience that God is leading him, and that with God's leadership there are no mistakes.

Therefore, again, stay anchored in your practice of meditation, that it will lead you higher and higher into the inner reality of self, whose core is peace, on the ultimate plane of life. When you find that perpetual peace within self you will also have obtained the ability to maintain the same.

David: Saint Germain, you just mentioned that there are things around us that we have no control over, like invasions of other countries. How do you masters in the spirit world manifest in this kind of environment or situation?

The Work of the Soul

We are protected by a ring of fire. Not fire as you know it on earth, but by God's love. We can go into any environment and we are not hurt. We are not bothered by it. We are protected. But that did not come by God's grace alone. It came by working with our mental and emotional energies on earth, by which we learned how *not* to allow lower frequencies to come into our frequency, much as you would learn how to turn the dial on a radio to move toward what you wanted to hear and away from what you did not want to hear. It is that kind of science, you see.

You can raise your frequency through meditation, by going inward. There's not just sitting meditation. There's walking meditation. There is also the kind of meditation you did tonight—centering upon one-pointed thinking. And that focus is what brings you away from the earth plane into self.

So we are not bothered at all by fear or inadequacy. Also, there is a great force of us—many millions—and we can band together when we need to in any situation to make any alterations in the human condition that is guided by Higher Intelligence.

You are building that ring of fire around yourselves by the work you're doing. Don't ever think that this is extracurricular work; this is the work of the soul. Each of you is doing it in your individual way. And your path is *your* path. That knowledge which you gain—incrementally at times, yes, and sometimes in great abundance—is God speaking to you through you, guiding you. Therefore, do not compare one life to another.

But there are certain essential tools which all need to use in order to come home. There is a *path* to follow. There are conditions to make. But since God is in charge, just look at what's ahead of you. And there on your path, the condition, the situation that is necessary will appear. The more you do that, the easier will your life become, remembering there are no mistakes, only learning and growing.

This is Samuel.

Yes.

Could you speak to your personal biography while you were on the earth plane? In terms of when and where you were born, how you came to be, who you became in terms of the masters, the teachers that might have assisted in you becoming, and how you came to want to be a master in the time that you were most prominently known to have existed?

The Earthly Life of Saint Germain

Does anyone here have about five or six hours? [Laughter.] Yes, we notice the complexity of his thinking. This just may keep him away from the top of the Mountain! [Laughter.] He has his own rainfall and snowfall in his mind, in the details, the nitty gritty of life.

I, Saint Germain, like Jesus, am like you. That is, we are human. We took on a human form. But at the same time, we are divine. Each of you is also divine. But so is this table which is in front of us, divine. The light in this room is divine. The windows, the doors, the roof, the earth, the plants—everything is divine, having come from One Energy. This fact I knew at a very young age.

Was I born into royalty? Yes. But royalty in those days was different from royalty today. That is, it was not based upon wealth for wealth's sake, nor show for show's sake. Rather it was based upon nobility of character. And that is what I sought to do with my life: to become a noble character.

Much like this instrument through whom I am speaking, I was also visited at a very young age by those from a former age, particularly from the era of Greek history in its beginning. People like Aristotle and Plato, Socrates. Those were the wise men of that age. And out of their thoughts came higher and higher thoughts. God used the evolution of thought through that plane, through that pathway.

There [in Greece] you find the most beautiful architecture ever designed. Classical architecture you call it now. It came out of minds that were very much in touch with the higher spheres of the spiritual world. That's why it has lasted through the ages, is still considered the most beautiful, and called "classic."

I was protected. Not so much by anyone knowing who I was; even I did not know that in the way that I know it now. But I was protected by the environment in which I lived. Being of the noble class, there was always someone in attendance. My major concern was not that of being attended. In fact, I disliked another person laboring for me. If there was someone scrubbing floors beside me, I would get down and scrub floors, too.

I had an insatiable curiosity about everything. Therefore, I was what you call, in your modern vernacular, a "whiz" at chemistry and math, astronomy, and astrology. These things seemed to come to me just naturally. But even as I am overshadowing Philip now, so I was overshadowed, too. I had certain gifts of my own, certain abilities and inclinations; certain things I derived from just being me, and they began to manifest. This is not something you can pre-design or pre-decide. So God placed me in an environment where I could grow freely in a protected way and thrive.

My entrance into European society was only part of my life. As I learned how to consciously leave my body at a very young age, I constantly went between the physical and spiritual worlds to be trained, to learn, to talk to the masters there, those that are of the ancient times of whom you on earth have no awareness. Only when you come here will you be able to have that experience.

When you are with them it is as if you're standing in the very presence of God himself. These beings are not mindful of self, they're mindful of one thing: God—God's will; God's love; God's care; God's healing tenderness; God's sweet and soft heart; God's justice and strong heart.

When you're in the midst of these masters, a rare few, you then understand your own inadequacy, your own need to discipline yourself, to gain mastery over your senses on every level, and to acquire higher and higher knowledge on the ladder of spiritual progress.

So I did that, and also I traveled around the world. I would materialize solidly in other parts of the world to learn languages, to study the customs of people, or sometimes just to have an adventure. People did not know that I was out of my body solidified as a spirit. But my life, as recorded in history, is primarily of my work in Europe, particularly in France.

How I Learned of Life

That [time] was exceedingly frustrating for me. There were many wonderful and noble people, noble in character. By contrast—as man got further and further away from the Author of Life—there came a stench into human character and spirit that was appalling. It was based primarily upon selfishness and greed—those two culprits that rob us of our self-esteem and our nobility.

So the wealthy only got wealthier and accumulated more as the poor got poorer. It is not dissimilar from your present environment here in this country. The foundations of *this nation* are not shaking for naught. Nor have those of great wealth, and those handling great wealth, been caught in the misuse of their money accidentally. All of this is the hand of God. But they will learn. They will come out on the other side. We need not condemn them or judge them any more than I did not in my time.

Having attained the higher planes of realization, I could see the movement within mankind, locally and worldwide, as being nothing more and nothing less than the design of God. Therefore, I was never disillusioned; I never judged anyone. I was never disappointed. But much as you would watch a film in a modern cinema today, I sat back and just watched it and learned. I learned so much.

The Master Jesus was greatly participating in my existence. Not as you know him. But as a being far, far removed from your explanations of him today, manifesting sheer joy, and sometimes great laughter, over the predicament found in those organizations named after him, saying at times, "They have nothing to do with me. It is their design, it's their idea. But they must go through it until they wake up. It also is a part of the great plan of God."

He [Jesus] would say to me, "When on earth, I so much appreciated the light, for my life was filled with much darkness. And when the night was over and the morning sun would rise, I would feel such peace and joy." And thus it is in the contrast of life—where life is filled with suffering, the suffering ends, and peace begins—that one can appreciate peace so much more.

Samuel, I could tell you many stories. I could speak at great length. I wanted to give you some of this inside personal view. And I'm sure that it has been edifying. It is the first time that I have spoken in this way to anyone. But it is time.

Samuel: Will you take a follow up question?

Yes, I will.

You mentioned that you were on the earth plane in the body, so you were born of woman, that is very clear. I'm curious though, because historically—

You *assume* that I was born of woman. Is it possible that there are things in God's creation you do not know?

Absolutely.

I leave that open for your exploration. You may continue.

Actually that's another great follow up question, but I guess the point of *this* question was, how long were you known to be in the body on the earth plane? Historically, it seemed to span several centuries. I just wanted to get confirmation from you.

Drawing Upon the Life Breath of God

Yes, and there are beings on earth today, particularly in the Far East, who live such illustrious and long lives. And being a master—understanding the essence of life, the elixir of life, that is, *what energy is and how that energy interfaces* with the human body and the human mind—I learned how to tap into that full time, all the time. To draw upon it. I learned what foods to use here on the earth plane to complement the heavenly energy, as it were, to make them work more proficiently within me. Do I make sense? [Yes.] It's an element I cannot describe to you at this point, but it's an elixir. I used that, plus my willfulness to live a long life, and not age.

You see, even here on earth, there are people who do not age, who remain rather young looking because the essence of their life is centered upon the Eternal night and day. They draw from that Source, even as there are people who are able to partake of that spiritual energy of which I partook, and of which you partake—exclusively so on their part—in which they do not need to eat or drink water. They are sustained, knowledgeably in some cases, and not in other cases, by the light and love of God as it flows into them.

They are special creatures sent to do that; to exemplify to others the presence of God. That is their life mission. They were born into this world as advanced souls to be able to do that. They did not come to earth as common people, any more than you did, all of you. You would not be in this room if you were common people. Your destiny is higher than that. You are called to go beyond that. Did I answer your question?

Yes, you did. Although it begs another, from your previous statement. You had said that I assume you were born of woman, and that got me thinking, because in the past I have asked you a similar question, many readings ago. At that time you had made a statement that you, in fact, were *not* woman-born. And that led me to believe that you were

an angelic being of some nature that somehow manifested on the earth plane, and that explained to me how you could have maintained your presence for such a long period of time.

Yes; that does not negate the possibility.

Anything is possible.

You Are Not Different From Me

You see, there are certain things that I am not ready to disclose, that mankind is not ready to hear. Not in some evasive way do I say this, but because these are things for a future, future life. Mankind as a whole has not evolved high enough, far enough, that there are enough of you to bring this information to earth fully and completely.

You yourselves are angelic in nature. Whenever you love unconditionally, that's the love of an angel. There are many labels. There are many projections onto all of us about who we are.

I'm no different than you in this sense, that my essence is the God Presence, the I AM. Just as you are the I AM. The angels are also the manifestation of the I AM Presence. They simply do not take a physical body, and as you well know, their role is different.

God comes to earth each time a human being is born. Imagine, with me, that you are the radiation of God come to earth in this physical body you call you. You are not different from me.

This is Mia.

Yes, Mia.

Is there religion in spirit world? For example, if somebody devoted their life concerned with a religion, and after they enter the spirit world, do they have to stay in that religion?

And The Greatest Of These...

Are there people leaving churches on earth? Yes. Actually, in droves, from what we can see! [**Laughter.**] And why do they leave? Because they wake up. They realize they have been eating *pablum* when they could be eating steak. So they leave, out of hunger. They want more. They realize that what they have been fed was good at one level. But where they are headed and according to their hunger, it is not now enough to adequately satisfy their spiritual appetite. And so they leave.

Here in spirit, as on earth, when you awaken to your hunger for more of life or the need to progress, you begin to take steps to eliminate the hunger and advance yourself. The hunger of the soul is the same in spirit as it on earth. It calls your attention to the need for more or something else in your spiritual diet. Having awakened, you search to find what it is that you are needing. However, there is a difference in spirit. How? There is a reason God placed the human spirit in a physical body. They are to mutually serve each other, each giving to the other some element not possible *without* the other. Call it "an exchange of *specialized* energies."

When you leave your body that specialized energy, flowing from the body to the spirit, is gone for good. And of course the reason the body becomes totally lifeless, when the spirit leaves, is that—while the body still retains a mass of cellular and atomic level energy for a time—it is missing the specialized energy supplied by the spirit and becomes "dead."

At the same time, this rarified energy, coming from the body to the spirit, is now cut off from the spirit, and thus, the spirit cannot grow as it once could on earth. Yes, by returning to the earth plane and helping others—while still in spirit—one can derive a certain amount of energy for the continuation of the growth of his spirit-self. Also, by service to others, in the spirit world, there is some measure of spiritual growth that does take place. But not nearly to the degree possible while embodied on earth.

Finally, as you are when you come to spirit, so you tend to remain. In other words, if you have not awakened on earth through higher understanding, you are not likely to be awakened in spirit either. For example, if you believe in a certain way, whatever your religious convictions, you will continue here in the same beliefs until enough time passes and based upon merit, God's grace can descend to you and begin the awakening process. Otherwise, your belief system remains the same.

Please understand that a fixed mind creates a fixed spirit. What you are emotionally and mentally (both comprising the spiritual state) when you die, you are fixed at in spirit. For this reason individuals can remain locked into archaic practices for many thousands of years in spirit. There are those who still live as if it were the 18th century, in the world of spirit, even though today, by your earthly calculations, this is the 21st century!

Then we say whatever your greatest love is on earth, is the thing that you are drawn to here. Therefore, you must be careful what you love. That is why we say, love God above all, who is highest and inmost.

Where is he inmost? In you. How can you experience him? By going inside. Yes, observing him indirectly outside, but observing him interiorly within self. You are the temple of God. If you want to know God, know yourself, know your own mind; know the presence of God through experience. Then when you come here, you will not be locked into any other love but the highest of highest of loves.

So many in spirit continue as they did on earth practicing their religion blindly, ignorantly. Until one day, when it is their time—by the design of God—they look up, and what they saw before no longer looks the same. Then they begin to question. Of course, we master teachers visit these individuals; we are drawn to them because we are to assist in awakening them. That's what we do as part of our job. We may whisper into their ear or give them a vision, or cause them to visit some portion of their own mind to reflect and ask questions within self. In this way, gradually they wake up and say, "Enough." And they look for higher vistas, new answers, higher answers. Did I answer your question?

Yes. I have another question. After they enter the spirit world can they spiritually grow?

Yes. Can they have a higher belief beyond their religion in spirit world?

Life's Progressions

This is not a static world where I am. Here we're more aware of progress than there on the earth plane. As God created life, there is always progress. Even if it's only incrementally. That is the nature of God; that is your nature. It is your nature to progress. So, the little mind asks little questions. Then that little mind begins to expand, little by little, and starts asking bigger questions.

The child doesn't ask the question, "Who is God?" He or she may if they are more advanced as a soul, but more likely they ask, "What are we going to have for dinner tonight?" or, "Can we go here or there?" The adult asks the higher level questions.

In the spirit world there's always progression, even if only an nth degree and over long periods of time, compared to what time it would take on earth. There is always the effort within the human soul itself—where God lives—to go forward, higher and higher. God created both the illusion of life—the waking dream—and the compelling desire to wake up from the dream. It is much like when you lie down to sleep you purposely do so. On the other hand, you do not intend to sleep forever so you set the alarm clock to wake you up. You intend to sleep and you intend to wake up. You consciously make provision for both.

When the Creator of us all, put himself under the sleeping spell or illusion of this life, he did so for the very purposes of what he—through you and me—can derive from this life. However, he also intended to awaken from the *sleeping spell.* This *intention* in all of us is manifested in our conscious and unconscious desire to progress. And through this progression we will eventually come to that time when we will be completely awake again to realize, "I am God! I fell asleep as I intended. Now! I am fully awake as I also intended. Story over!" And that, dear friends, is a part of the creative principle of God. It is all a part of God's great plan.

That's why we say there are no mistakes; be very patient; life is progressive, it goes in stages, there is such a thing as growth, and there's no such a thing as *not* growing, not awakening, not progressing.

Any guidance from spirit world for me? This is Annie.

Fully Realizing. . .You!

Yes. One of your guides standing by me who's touching the nose of Philip [laughter] is a small guide who's trying to make contact with you. Not a child, but a person taking on the guise of a child. And it is your mother who comes tonight in this way to say: "When you want the answers, return to that place of innocence, before you knew anything, before you believed anything. That place is in the interior of your mind and your heart. And it is like a blank slate upon which God the Father within you and the Mother within you writes the answers to your life.

You can obtain much knowledge which can grow into wisdom by this methodology. Just let go of all things, all beliefs, all creeds, all concepts. Just become totally blank, totally open."

Your mother and others will bring the answers to you. You are there to a great extent already. But sometimes, your ideas, your thinking, connected to the earth plane and former experiences, those like everyone, block you. Get past them. Not by fighting them, or trying to overcome them, or by laying them down. Open up, like the flower that opens to the sunlight, and just receive. Grow more and more into that spiritual stance, that spiritual posture, and you will realize more fully who you are, what you are, and where you are going.

Saint Germain, this is David.

Yes, David.

How different is Philip as a channel in relationship to other people who channel you?

How different?

I know some people channel through writing and some type at the computer, but of other people who channel, there are a number of other people who say they channel you.

The Essence of Dedication

When I first came to Philip, I came through the instrument you know of as trumpet, which is just a [megaphone like] means of conveyance for us to focus our energy on the earth plane and magnify it. I said to him that I was so happy to come to someone as dedicated as he is. He continued—in the midst of much turmoil, in the midst of deprivation, in the midst of great questioning and self-doubt, in the midst of the indifference of many, and the criticism of some.

He was, as it were, swinging to and fro between depression and great joy. But he listened. He followed. Again and again, he returned to that place that he knew as a child, that place of innocence, where he called God his Heavenly Father. He listened intently, for unlike many people who walk through this life, who seem to just have an easy way and things just seem to come to them, it was not so for him. But had that happened [had things come easily], he could not be the person he is today, doing what he does.

Few know the real inner burdens that he carries. But he is ever turning them over, and turning them over; talking to me. Sometimes calling me in or Jesus, or any other beings that he feels impressed to call in at the moment, and asks them to help him. Of course, he calls upon God.

When you work this way, around the clock with Spirit, when you seek to devote your life in the face of many, many obstacles—some of your own making, perhaps—you gain a great amount of merit and a great opening to the sphere of Spirit; yours and ours. And then we can pour into you something that is extraordinary.

There's no question in my mind that as you watch this portrayal of my presence here, some of you attached to your earthly concepts say, "Well, I look at him and he still looks like himself. I hear a tonality in his voice that sounds like he does. Is this not just the overshadowing of his own self with his self?"

You are all channels. But the energies that come through you are very subtle. You detect them *not* because you do not know how to attune to them as he does. Does this make him superior? No. Any more than someone who practices piano diligently is not different than one who does not.

The difference is in the practice, and the diligence applied. So where he is skilled in this fashion, you are skilled in another. It is his calling, and you have your calling.

Whatever you are drawn to, put yourself to the task, and be dedicated toward it, in the most focused way. For it is where God has placed you to realize yourself, just as my medium is realizing himself.

As far as the difference between him and others, the most noted difference is *dedication*.

Lynn: I have one more question. Following on Sam's inquiry into your biography—

Yes.

I've been assuming that because of your spiritual stature, you may have evolved beyond the need or the desire to incarnate on the earth plane again; but maybe I'm assuming too much. Do you, might you, incarnate again?

I am, right this moment. Why should I want otherwise? [**Laughter.**] Because I am able to go between your world and the world in which I exist in reality all the time, why should I want to come back to the earth plane?

That's what I was thinking—because you can work with many, many people now, in a way that you couldn't when you were on earth physically.

You have answered your own question.

Visitations

Not only that, but should I come back into another earthly body, what is to guarantee that I could have the privilege of being able to convey truth the way I am here tonight? Albeit, it is more difficult in some ways to get into the consciousness of this being called Philip than it would be to get into the womb of a woman. Meaning, it is easier to work directly with the physical body that you are controlling than the physical body of another who allows you to control it. Do I make sense? [**Yes.**]

But that's not my calling. I've done enough on earth; I'm not seeking to return except in this way. And this is not the second coming. There are many comings happening night and day. Back and forth, back and forth, back and forth. And some of those are individuals visiting each of you, doing the same work that I'm doing with Philip.

If right this moment we could remove the blindness caused by lack of experience, it would reveal the sphere of people surrounding you now from the spirit world. You would be totally, totally shocked. You would not believe how many hundreds and hundreds of spirits surround this circle now. Those who came with me are from various levels in the spirit world.

Some were brought by master teachers who are letting the people they are in charge of and helping watch and listen, that they may learn. Some are seeking to do the thing that I do—a master teacher seeking to enter into the body of someone. Or someone seeking to help an inventor. You know all this. I need not repeat it.

But I'm enjoying myself. Not many people allow this kind of entrance for such a great length of time, nor with such quality of conveying the truth. It is the training which Philip received here in the spirit world as a child when going out of his body, yes, but also he did due diligence—his studying and absorbing, learning, practicing certain teachings, universal teachings. In this way, he provided the right kind of environment, the right kind of atmosphere. None of this was by accident, but all by design. So it is with your life. **(I)**

Saint Germain, this is Richard.

Yes, Richard.

My first question is, what is the spirit world like? I have read about it, but I'd like to hear about it from Saint Germain.

Which part do you want to hear about? It is so vast.

The most obvious part. [Laughter.]

You're talking about the realms of glory, are you not?

The higher realms, yes.

The Higher Realms of God's World

Your imagination could never do it justice. There is no way that you could appreciate even the light. It is so brilliant because that realm is made of light itself, pure light. And the presence of God in that sphere, that endless sphere, is so palpable. When you're in that area of life with God, you become an expanded being. You realize how small your life was. How narrow is this body cavity.

And some of those who [while sleeping at night] come here [in an out-of-the-body experience], complain that they must return to their physical body and don't want to. They say, "Do I have to go back to the physical world? Do I have to go into that narrow space of my body again? I don't relish going back to into that harsh and dense atmosphere—that vibration of the earth plane!"

In those realms, all is love, all is light. And in that space, you can have whatever you want. It's up to you, because at that point, you are a co-creator with God. That is what Saint Germain does—I am a co-creator!

You have heard that I am in charge of the Violet Light or the violet ray—the purple light, the golden light. Yes, I come in those lights, the gold and purple lights. As a master, I am allowed to use the radiation of God's energy to direct it for his purposes, by his will, towards individuals and situations where it is called for.

If you could see this room now, there is a radiation of violet light, a canopy of light over the room. I brought that. I have that kind of power, though I don't speak of it often. For I am never interested in impressing you with me. I'm interested in impressing you with the Father, who sends me; the one in whom I dwell, and who dwells in me.

In that region, there is a holy council. I cannot describe it in earthly terms, but we meet. All the ones who have mastered life, who understand the cause and effect, the principles of self-mastery meet in consultation. If it's the core group, then it is less numbers. If it is all the masters, it is a great, great number.

As I said in a previous communication, man is far older than you have been able to calibrate. And only recently there has been a discovery by which they now calibrate that man is something like 380 million years old. Can you imagine how many civilizations have come and gone on the face of the earth? Can you imagine how many people are here resultant from that?

So you have little understanding of how vast the spirit world is and how many people there are. When I speak of the gathering of many masters, then I am speaking of that realm. In the highest areas.

In the lesser areas, life is pretty much as it is here on earth. There are cities and towns, there are churches, there is green grass and flowers and birds; all in a rarefied way, do they manifest! But there is great joy. Great laughter. The smile which you see on Philip's face is my smile.

Prepare yourself to go to those realms, to that space, to total oneness with God. What I have spoken earlier regarding longing for God and seeking to be with God—just to be with God—will take you there. These realms are filled with those kinds of people.

I could not come and use Philip if he had not, from childhood and prior to that, had that personal relationship with

God. He says he was born knowing God. It is true because we took him out of his body. Prior to entrance into this body, he had experiences where he knew God personally. He came into this expression with that. And so it follows him wherever he goes. And because of the similarity of my experience with his, though there are many other aspects to it, I'm able to use him. Without that essential element, without that core truth of his being, I would not have been able to use him.

I said to him in the beginning that I was so happy to come to someone as dedicated as he is. That dedication's fulcrum point is based upon a deep and sincere love for God and appreciation of God's presence in his life. He still does give thanks, turning again and again to the Father in the midst of daily work, and saying, "Thank you," often with tears in his eyes. He never expected in his life to ever be used in this way, or to achieve anything of this kind of value. Rather, he had the opposite feeling of himself. That came from his upbringing on earth and from his family's situation. But slowly and gradually we revealed a broader reality.

So those of us—going back to your question, Richard—who come to work in this fashion and on this level, at this depth, come from that realm, that highest of highest realms—the summit as I call it—to the Mountain of Life.

And I could just say so many, many, many things about the spiritual world, but we have to reserve some, because we want you to have some surprises when you come here.

Saint Germain, this is David. You mentioned that there was a hierarchy of—

[Saint Germain broke out in laughter.] He says "David" so offhandedly, as if his name did not belong to him! Yes, my son?

Well, I almost forgot to identify myself, that's why I did it…

You often forget to identify yourself!

David (smiling): Because I *am* the world! I am all people! You mentioned the holy council and the core group. Can you say more about the spirit world government?

Governing by Love

It is vast. You think here with your modern computers that you're able to run your government pretty efficiently now, pretty effectively. When you go online, you call it "going online,"—we talk about it as "touching in with the frequency,"—it's the same idea; when you touch in with the frequency on your electric computer, you find that you're able to go through file after file, or site after site, for much information.

We have had computers in the spirit world for thousands of years. Not as you think of them, but the mind here acts as our computer. Since the mind is limitless, there are masters who have their entire mind filled with volumes and volumes and volumes of information that they can access at the twinkling of an eye. And they can send it faster than you can send a message from one computer to another through the electric wire.

Through this system, that is mind-to-mind communication, we have perfect governing. For as you can send one message from one central computer to many thousands of computers, so the master of any realm can send one thought to the minds of millions in a nanosecond (one billionth of a second). And they, not being limited, can all assemble in a nanosecond, as well. First they were not there; in a nanosecond, they all now appear in an assembly hall for a talk. Or in the woods for a picnic. Or somewhere for a party or just to be together. Even without gathering, the master of such a realm can communicate his words and affections to all and all at the same time!

When such a master—as orchestrated by the Father—leads in this way, the people of that spiritual realm feel greatly and equally loved; the governing is made so very easy and everyone is happy. It is in the higher realms where all are able to connect and identify with the Heavenly Father's will uniformly that such universal communication and governing is possible. In this way, governing in the spirit world is very proficient and highly, unmistakably effective.

We never have to sleep in spirit. There's always someone on watch, so to speak. Someone always overshadowing and helping. And it's all out of love, you see. All orchestrated by divine love, which is another word for unconditional love. Love is the reigning principle. No one is elected here. Everyone is, in fact, volunteering so much, that if it were on earth, there is no way any of your computers could handle all the requests.

But we have a place for everyone. There is no place where one cannot be used or find a place to work. Imagine! There are millions and millions of people coming to the spirit world at all times, some are out of their bodies and remain connected [to their body on earth], coming and going. When your nation in this hemisphere goes to sleep at night, how many millions of people do you think there are floating in space? How many of them are not just hovering above their body remaining connected by the silver cord, but are coming out into the ethers with us?—in consultations, in meetings, meeting loved ones who have died, meeting a child who passed, who did not even grow on earth. Coming here just to walk in the fields, to observe the flowers and the grass. To be electrified by the energies that are here; to be revivified to come back to the earth plane; awakening refreshed but not knowing why or how.

We are governing all of that. At all times. In all places. There are countless master teachers helping each one on earth master their life. And so there is a grand hierarchy well orchestrated, well directed, working in perfect order. And if there is some lack of understanding, there is no harsh judgment. We never give to anyone something which they cannot do or cannot learn to do, for we can discern immediately who this person is, what their capability is, what they would vibrate with as an assignment. We would never put a clumsy man (one who was clumsy on earth with children) in a house with spirit children. Not that he could not learn, but we would put in charge of children a woman or man who had loved children, who was good at working with children, taking care of children, whose affections were highly developed; were not only personal, but universal; he or she could see in any child, themselves; and treat every child as their own. Those are the master teachers.

I see you as my own. There's not one of you here I don't feel as my own. That means I have that kind of love within me, to love you. I see you as myself. There is no differentiation.

Therefore, there is no hindrance to love you, to hold back love, to not love you. Even in your worst times, I would not stop loving you.

But it is the Father in all of us, including you, that has come and given that kind or caliber of love and the capacity to love in that way. As you go up the Mountain, as you go up the rungs of life's ladder, you cannot help but develop your love in a broader and broader way, without which total unconditional love cannot manifest in you.

Some of you may think, "I asked him one question, but he answered about a dozen." [**Laughter.**] Yes, this is my nature, in part, but it's also…please understand that this door doesn't open very often. I waited a long time to find an individual, and I am not just wanting to hear myself talk. I know these words are going to go out to thousands and thousands of people.

When I have a chance to educate, I educate. That's my purpose in coming. It's not to exchange small talk. It's not to talk about the instances, or incidences in your life. You can take care of those things. But it's my job to try to pave the way ahead of you so you can walk more easily, so you can be inspired more highly. So you can understand more precisely, to make the way easier.

Saint Germain does not come to you because out of some fickle reason I'm responding to you; no, you're here because we see your potential, and you have merit already. Otherwise, you could not be sitting here.

I orchestrated who would be sitting here. I inspired Philip as to who should be included in this circle. It is a small circle because the caliber of people that are needed for this work—this work, meaning the AIM work, the work which he does—takes a very, very high caliber individual who is intelligent, who loves, who is able to be expanded, who takes directions easily, who does not take personally each thing that happens.

You must be people of faith, above all. Faith. Here I am, speaking through this man. And you're sitting here with baited breath. Most people would think you're crazy, to hang your life upon one person sitting, talking, bringing forth truths. No, you're a people of faith. That's why you're here.

But faith is also accompanied by a childlike nature, and you have that, too. And so, David, to get back to your question about the governing of the spirit world, now you have it all. And then some! **[Laughter.]**

Saint Germain is in a rare mood today. Why? Because Philip has gone through things which you know not of, and progressions. Some of you who know him intimately can see this. There is a change in his demeanor, a lightness in step. And as the medium goes, so I am able to go, or come—whatever you may say.

Saint Germain, this is Sam.

I know this—I know those tones.

I would like to—

Those mellow tones of this young man. This old soul young man. Now, what did you want to say?

I know I did touch upon what David asked you…

133

I did not say enough?

Well, no, this is kind of like another unique question, and you don't have to go that far into it, but...

Oh, now he's telling the master what he can and can't do! [Laughter.]

Well, let me put my Roswell cap on, and ask you...

Yes, go ahead.

When you talk about masters, versus when you were talking about the supreme council, or the core council...since we're human beings, we assume spirit world primarily consists of people or beings who were once formerly human. Is that a false assumption?

[Saint Germain smiles] I'm listening to them laugh here in the spirit world.

Divine Laws

No. It is not a false assumption. Earth is made up of human beings. The government of the spirit world is on many levels, even as you have here the county level, the state level, the regional level, and then the national level. If the earth was existing as idealized, there would be the world level government.

We do not seek to dominate or control anyone. We're all under divine law. Therefore, we're all under divine direction. The more the circumference of understanding, the greater the height we can go in the spirit world, and the more we know for ourselves what we must or need to do. There is no dictation. Orders are often handed down by thought. Not by word, but by thought. A flash of a voice across space, as you would call it here on earth, would direct someone to do this or that next, without anyone having to appear.

The Grand Council is made up of human beings who have lived on earth, but so many of them are not the people you would expect. Not that some of them are not a part of it, but it includes people millions of years old—not just hundreds or thousands, but millions! I spoke of them prior to this in my last talk with you, in which I said when you stand in their midst, you feel the presence of God to such an extent, you seek to examine yourself. And you are humbled by their presence.

They are the Grand Council. They are the ones who do not necessarily participate in some kind of group meeting, in some kind of "physical appearance" as this. But they are emanating their energies across the plains of humanity. They are the closest companions, so to speak, of God. They're the ones who are able to *be* him, to radiate out his energies most specifically and fully.

I participate in part of that. But I am not allowed to give all the details. There is the angelic world—to finish answering your question—participating in this, also. They do not govern, but carry out directives, and intermingle with us humans, to serve and to carry out the Council's directions.

It is the Father's will and the Father's way that in the end there need be no government, as you know it on earth. Each person needs fully be in oneness with God, as I have described many times. If each had this oneness with God, the divine will would be known at all times and by all people. Then no government would be necessary. That is the ultimate ideal, even here on earth, but especially here in Spirit.

Our coming together here is not done often; not in the way of your thinking. But we are always together, thought to thought, heart to heart, through the energies which we are passing back and forth. And we can tune into each other, and gain insight and counseling if we need more information. From where I stand, I can know so much by one glimpse, one tuning in.

Because I am multi-dimensional—even as I am here with Philip at this time, I'm also able to tune into other people in various spheres, overseeing them, helping them—I am not just here and only here at this moment. That is the capability of the ultimate master teacher.

I want to add to this one final thing, and that is: when we talk about being a "master," I want to put this in context. The first grader masters first grade work, so he becomes a master, does he not? The fifth grader, the sixth, the seventh, the twelfth. They're all masters in their own right. So mind you, when we talk about "masters," we're talking about masters at different levels. Among those who make up the ultimate council in Spirit I spoke of, not all are supreme masters, or ultimately "arrived." Not all are at that level. Obviously, Saint Germain is still working on his soul, too. For he is here learning, as well; he is also working on his need to give, as well.

Tim: Saint Germain, I am just dying to know—is there a number of how many beings make up the Grand Council?

You may need to die first to know! [**Laughter.**] Next question, please.

Saint Germain, this is Jewel.

Yes, Jewel.

Your words about the spirit world are so touching, and the energy is so, so much about love. I have been experiencing, as I sit here, the presence of so many of those souls that have passed over in this war [Iraqi war]. I feel their presence and a feeling from them, such a great—just a great love. You know, as I witness this world and I see what is happening, I know many are praying for peace. And yet so many souls are hating us, are just hating. And that is *their* prayer.

Yes.

I just am asking if you can help us see it from your perspective, and to understand what is this about, where is it going, and will the love, the prayers that come from a place of love, ultimately help heal these people that are so filled with hatred and have peace?

Living Life's Lessons

No one hates but what they don't hurt themselves. You know this. And so hate ultimately always teaches us *not* to hate. [**Yes.**]

But some are so filled with fear, that that contagion of fear underlines the energy of hate and amplifies it. Often we dislike what we cannot control. In this case, many lives have been terribly torn up. There is a fear. Where shall I get food? How shall I feed myself? What is going to happen to this land?

But you see—as I and many have said—nothing happens that the Father does not allow. If you are here in this circle by virtue of merit from the past, either in this life or in former lives, then you are here, and you are not there. If, on the other hand, your karmic path called for you to be an Iraqi person [in the midst of war], you would be there. And you would be undergoing those sufferings.

Each person is moved on the chessboard of life by the hand of God, whether they are wounded in war, wounded in love, whether they live a natural life on earth, whether they are rich or poor, no matter the circumstance. Each one is under the guidance of God's personal, invisible, quiet, intercessory power as it streams to and through all mankind, both on earth and in the spirit world. And there are countless numbers of spirit guides working to help carry out the will of the Father, as well.

You see, in the story he wrote for each person, there is a script to be fulfilled, that each one who undergoes whatever they undergo, learns their lesson. And those who are observant do learn their lesson.

Is there some object lesson to be learned in your country's going to war with Iraq at this time? Some of your people are very set against it; some are for it. What is to be learned? Is it that war *does* or *does not* pay? As you and I see any of life's situations—personal or global—it is according to our script.

Teaching my medium to be most objective and detached, I told Philip, "I want you, my son, to draw away from too much interaction with the war in Iraq. It is not your plight, nor your life. It is not happening to you, and it's not really happening to them. They are but emanations of God come to earth, experiencing their life as it unfolds. And from their life they will or will not learn. But in ultimate reality, it is God's learning. For there is no birth, and there is no death. There is only learning and growing, and all is God."

You [Jewel] are feeling the presence of individuals around you; it is true. There are many. There are several dozen around you. Partly, you have drawn them to you out of your great empathy, your compassion. Partly, they are there because they want to bask in this energy. Not all know about this opportunity, but those who are ready for it are aware. Some were brought here by the masters to learn so they can make full transition. They are here listening to Saint Germain. I brought some of them, and there are many thousands around you that you do not even see or hear or sense. They are as in a stadium watching all of this.

How long will it [the war] go on? As long as it will go on. That script is in the hands of God, not in my hands. Each one must play their role; each role must be played out. The purpose for which your country went into that land must be fulfilled.

You would all do well to read the *Bhagavad Gita* to study about Krishna and Arjuna, and gain a deep understanding of what is being expressed there, symbolically. Krishna and Arjuna, on the deepest level, represent the mind. Arjuna says, "No, I do not want to go into battle. Those are my relatives." And Krishna says, "It is God's will. You are not doing this battle, he is. Have courage. Have faith."

God knows what he is doing. There are no mistakes. In this dream/nightmare [of life], it appears as if it is too awful. But unless the Father shows you what is too awful, you will not go for what is also wonderful. Do you understand what I mean?

Yes, I do.

Of course, this brings no comfort. It would be easy for me to say all of this in some philosophical, cheerful way. In no way do I make light of all this. For I have also said to you that we are here not for people who are awakened. We are here for those who are not awakened, and we must comfort them. We must help them up the Mountain. We must help them know what we know. And, therefore, missionary work is important. Working out among the people, educating them, helping them is important.

The Father uses all of this as an analogy. And so the relationship between Krishna, representing the Lord, and Arjuna, representing doubting Thomas, doubting man, faithless man, is what goes on in your mind at all times. It is a lesson for all, including for God. But it will not be until you come here that you will totally, completely comprehend this necessity. And, as I said through this medium as he quoted another individual, "God is having fun with you."

Those of you who have had nightmares—and there's no exceptions—who have awakened from them filled with fear or sweaty palms, are so glad that it was only that. That it was not really happening. When you first wake up, if it has a great hold on you, you feel, "Oh, it happened!" whatever it may be. If you killed someone [in your dream], you're so fearful, or someone's about to reveal a secret about you that you do not want revealed. As time passes, and you come into higher consciousness, more and more awake and out of the sleep state, you can begin to laugh and say, "That was nothing more than a nightmare. I am so glad it didn't happen."

That's how it will be when you come to the spirit world. But meanwhile, you have to know that you are living a life on earth as a character in a play written by God. Therefore, your life on earth is ultimately for the purpose of "waking up." You are asleep now, you see.

What is going on here this moment is your dream. It's God's dream in your mind. You have created these circumstances in which you have found these men and women sitting around you. But if you were to die right now, you would see this was all mind stuff. In the astral plane it exists because there, beings still believe it is all real, you see. That's why they come back to the earth plane and continue with their attachments; why they continue to carry out their life almost as it was on earth.

From whence I come, there is no illusion. We can see it as the movie of God, playing out on the screen of life. You are characters passing through this light. But you are created by God. Sleep on that for a while and see how it sounds and feels to you. Examine it closely. And try to put yourself in a place where you can also see from the higher perspective. If you follow what we are teaching you, that's where you'll finally arrive.

David: Saint Germain, in relationship to that question, you previously said that masters can intercede to alter the human condition from time to time as guided by higher intelligence. Are you intervening in the Iraq situation now?

Masters, All

In part. But there are others who are responsible for that radiation of light. I am more on the end of receiving individuals here. That is the group, the organization I work with. But a master at a higher elevation of accomplishment, just like here on earth, is capable of doing a number of things at one time, is multi-faceted. It's one of the reasons that Philip Burley could be used: he is multi-faceted.

Those of you who have watched him see him do a number of things, and see he is talented in a number of areas. So am I. And so I not only sometimes drop in on the battlefields there, but I come in [to the earth plane] this way, and I'm also conducting other responsibilities. What you hear of Saint Germain is only a small portion [of my activities]. As you bask in the sunlight, you are only touched by a small portion of it. Do I make myself clear? [Yes.]

Saint Germain is more than the sum total of what you are presently experiencing here. But so are you, in the expanded version of yourself. You think of yourself as you see yourself in the mirror. As you conduct your life through whatever work you do, as to foods you favor, etc. You identify yourself with all those things. I don't. I identify myself with cosmic thought. Cosmic living. Limitless living. I have the ability, as you do, to be multi-faceted. I can express all kinds of emotions, all kinds of thoughts. I can take on all kinds of personalities, if I so desire.

Are you not made in the image and likeness of God? [**Yes.**] Then look at how many facets there are of God. And if you're going to reach the totality of who you are, you're going to realize you, too, have many, many characteristics you have not even begun to touch in with, let alone, know about.

Are my answers at all helpful today? [**Yes.**] Do you believe them? [**Yes.**] You need to test them, against the backdrop of life experience. But you'll not find them wanting. I'm only jesting with you. Are you hungry?

David: For spiritual food? Yes.

We need not eat; we could donate this food to some charity, if you would like to just fast.

Samuel: I'd rather eat!

You would rather eat. Let's be sure and publish that! Here's one of profundity who would rather eat [earthly] food than get spiritual food. He is the one who asks all the questions of such deep and dire need. But he would rather eat.

Samuel: That's what the body needs, now.

Is that true? If I should give you a lobotomy, and you could not connect with your body, would you still be hungry? No, you would not, because it means you're connecting your thought to your body's feeling. But if you're a true master, you could cut off that thought, disconnect from feeling the body. And you could feed upon the energy of God within you, flowing in through what we call the third eye or the *medulla oblongata*. That's where I'm trying to take you.

As you know, I am just joking with all of you. I realize you're hungry.

Samuel: Whew!

This body I'm using is not hungry. Surprising, as much as I have used his energies. It is because there are extra energies here sustaining him today. On purpose. Because we're having a double, almost triple session, you see.

I have covered volumes and volumes of information here. But we have only, as you say on earth, "touched the tip of the iceberg." What a funny analogy. You have only touched in with a small portion of the spirit world, and the secrets, the mysteries, the truth. God bless you, enjoy your meal. I shall see you after you have supped. **(II)**

Jewel: Saint Germain?

Yes.

As I'm listening to what you're saying, I'm thinking about how each embodiment seems to have some kind of predetermined possibility, and that we're here to play a certain role in each lifetime, that we may learn certain things. I'm wondering what role prayer has in this dynamic? Because we all pray for things. We all pray for each other. We pray, but maybe our prayer isn't asking for the best thing. Maybe the best prayer of all is just that people find their highest expression of who they are.

Sometimes we think others are doing something which we might think is wrong, yet maybe they're meant to go through it. So, what is the best way to pray?

A Prayer Answered

First of all, to answer the first part of your question: for those who pray, it is in their script to pray. It is their concept that they can appeal to God and make changes by appealing. The better prayer, for many pray amiss, is the prayer of affirmation. What you need, God already knows. He never withholds it. When the time is right and you are ready for something, it comes. Witness the total cycle of life in which so many times things happen for you that you never ask for. Did you bring spring? Did you make the sunshine? Have you created the air, or caused the birds to sing or to fly? Did you create food or cause it to grow? There's so much that God does.

So, therefore, the most important prayer is the affirmation to the Father, "I thank you for what you are bringing me. What I need is on its way to me." In all things, God is ready, willing, and able to give to you what you *need*—and I underline the word *need*—when you have your hands and arms out. There are many on earth who never ever, ever utter a word of prayer. Yet they still prosper, demonstrating clearly that God is ever giving to everyone.

Live positively. Then you're living in the stream of God's life. Live in the light. Find your inner happiness, and don't let anyone take you away from that. Learn to smile under all circumstances, for it brings out of you the ever-present love, the ever-present joy of God. It is already in you, you see. How do you access it? Meditation is one way, but continue to affirm it by acting as if it's already so. That is a prayer answered.

Thus, when you go out to do something, act as if your prayer is already being answered. And if it is not, you shall know so, and the lesson will be learned. You may have gone for something you don't need, or it is not yet time for it to come to you. It has been said, when the pupil is ready, the teacher appears. That is true.

So there are many erroneous ideas on earth about spiritual practices. They vary greatly. Some are slight imperfections and some are gross misunderstandings. Those who think that they should offer up an animal for sacrifice in order to appease a God who really doesn't pay any attention to those kind of things but measures us by our heart, are praying amiss. Will their prayer be answered? Yes, if within it there can be found an element of praying for something they literally need. If not, it will not be. But at all times, God is in charge, God is providing—amply! *More* than amply.

Have you ever known any place on earth that ran out of oxygen or sunshine? Never. Everything is all within divine order. If it is given to you to pray in a certain way, whether it be after the Catholic fashion or Protestant fashion matters not to God. But when you pray, do not pray begging. He is your *Father*; he has everything waiting for you. "Father, I know you have for me what I need. Please help me to know what that is, and guide me to receive it." Then simply wait and he shall deliver—if, in fact, it is a genuine need and it is time for your character to receive it.

If you praise and thank God under all circumstances, you will grow in his grace. From all of life you are learning the lesson that it is *his* will, not your will, that is to be fulfilled. There is only one will.

David: So in regard to what you were saying earlier, in your comments about the war and prayer, is there a prayer that we should offer up about this war?

The Indelible Markings of Your Life Script

Pray! If you are so moved to pray for an individual, or the group, then you should do that. That is how you are moved. That is how God is using your image. Whether or not that prayer has power, is within God's hands. If he chooses to carry it forth as an energy you've put out to help someone, it shall happen. If it is an exercise for you to learn from, and the energy goes nowhere, that is for you.

The major thing is just trust God under all circumstances. Do the thing that you are moved to do on your path, as things appear. That is your role. That is your calling. That is what is indelibly marked within your script. Therefore, what do we say? What is the highest truth? To know thyself.

If you know yourself, then you know what role to play, how to act, where to go, what to do, what to be, what to ask for. Going inside consistently and regularly, you will come to know yourself. Finally, you will reach that level of self-awareness and spiritual growth in which you will ask for nothing. You will not seek for anything. You will just *be*. And all that you need will come to you. Master after master I have spoken to found—particularly when on earth—"When what we needed was needed, and if we were doing a righteous action or in a correct relationship with the living God, that would just flow to us. We didn't have to fight for it or beg for it. It came." It was the same for me.

When you live life and give out your energy to help others, that is the first step toward guaranteeing that your own needs will be met. It is in giving out that we receive the blessing. And the masters are those who have mastered life to such an extent that they realize the very thing I spoke of at the beginning of this afternoon: life is about climbing the Mountain, awakening to the reality, getting over the illusion and realizing that they are God. In that realization, what else is needed? Realizing they are God, they then are able to, what? They are able to apply the principles of God to get all that they need. And the number one principle is, if I give to others what they need, I will get what I need.

Saint Germain, this is Samuel again.

Yes.

What exactly does it mean to be righteous? In other words, if you look at life in the way that has been described, everyone is playing a defined role. You know, we're all scripted to do what it is that we are doing. In the case of Saddam Hussein, he is playing his role; he is doing what he is meant to do. The same way that Adolph Hitler did, and Stalin before him. So, in terms of a concept of righteousness, is that all that it is, just a concept, more or less?

Being, Awareness, and Bliss

Righteousness means to be in the right relationship with God. It is not in their script at present, nor was it in the script of Hitler, to even understand that. It was not in *his* script to understand that God is in charge, not Hitler. He tried to play the role of God. That's why he lost. But that was in his script. When he came to this side, he awakened greatly to the reality of what he had done, how he had been used, but there's a blessing for that, too. For *if* we are one of those individuals who came into a life expression over which we have no control, finding ourselves playing a certain role, then who is responsible? It is God.

The great awakening is that there is nothing happening. You must always return to that point. There is *nothing* happening. *There is nothing happening.* I am being! What does that mean? God is just *being*. In the silence of who God is, he's just being. Like the bird sitting on the limb. Quietly. Placidly. Peacefully. Not taking anything in, not giving anything out. Just being. Or the tree upon which the bird is sitting—it is just *being*.

As you look out this window in front of you, you can look at many objects. They are all just being. And they have varying degrees of awareness. The bird on the limb has more awareness than the tree does. But the tree, mark my word, has awareness. The mimosa tree, for example, has an awareness that's far more sensitive than most other trees—once you touch its leaves, it is so sensitive, it will close them. So it is with some other plants of such high level of sensitivity. The dog has more awareness than the bird. It becomes the friend to man. Human beings are the most aware, therefore, they are most like God, who is aware of everything.

So in the state of being, one may sense the energy by looking, by feeling. In looking and feeling, one becomes aware of other things. The child in the beginning is only "being." He lies in the crib; there he "be." He's only being. As he looks out into the world and his vision comes into greater perfection, his sensitivity and touch is more acute, and he becomes aware. So he goes from being to awareness. When you become aware of the greatest of the greatest thing—God's love, God's presence in you—that is bliss. So that's why we say we are "being, awareness, bliss."

Imagine the number of people around you, even in your neighborhood, who are not even aware of one ounce of what you know? Very few are aware. If they hear about *being, awareness* and *bliss* to them, it is gobbledygook. And so it is with Saddam Hussein. He is his own God. He cannot hear the voice of God. But, is he playing a role?

From our vantage point we see each one playing his or her role that humanity may learn what is good and what is evil. That they may shun evil and do only good. In this sense, the role of evil men on earth has driven many to long for and do only good. Why do good men want war no more? It is because they have faced the evils of war and the futility of it all. Perhaps they have learned the lesson that God has been trying to teach all humanity.

Establishing Your Foothold on the Mountain

In the ultimate sense of righteousness, the right relationship with God has to do with doing good. And so Hussein was chosen to do something which you would call *not* good, or "evil." Could he be an object lesson to humanity? For in each of us, we can find elements of a Saddam Hussein, *and* a Jesus Christ.

That is the object lesson. That is the purpose of all these individuals. And so what do we [from Spirit] say? We say, "Stay in your business, stay on your own path. "Be" what's on your path. It is your salvation, your resurrection you are seeking to earn."

Therefore, the Masters learned, as I did, to stay focused. Focused, focused, focused. Looking neither to the right nor the left. Always returning to establishing your foothold on the Mountain. And always climbing upward, higher and higher. Keeping your eye on the peak, on God. Only on God. Only on God. Over and over. Night and day, night and day.

God is real, you see. Until God goes from being a theory, or something outside of yourself, to God within you that you can feel, that you can experience, you will continue to dabble in this world; you'll continue to wander about, you'll continue to debate things. But I tell you when you finally realize that there is only One Energy, you will become silent and go inward. For *there* [inside your consciousness] is everything that you need. You will become, at least mentally, more and more of a recluse. We Masters spent much time by ourselves.

That's why Jesus spent so much time by himself. He knew these things. He didn't need to come forth and tell the people. He didn't need that for his soul. He was already arrived. He already knew how to multiply fishes and loaves, and to heal. He knew how to read minds, to look into the future, the past, to understand and discern the present. He was able to communicate with Moses and Elijah. His disciples, Peter, John, and James witnessed this fact.

He did all those things. He didn't need to do this for himself. He would rather have been by himself in his reverie of love with God, because everything else is an illusion.

The Bible tells us that we are the temple of God. We must realize this is fact and not just allegorical. Then go inside the temple of yourself and live there and meet God. All the energy manifested outward is all being drawn back to God. One day it may all disappear, be absorbed back into God, into the Ocean of Light that he is, the Divine Intelligence and the Divine Love that he is. And then the play may be over, the curtain dropped, and the stage disappear. God can do that if he wants to. He is the creator and the destroyer. That means he is the source of creation and he can also stop or transform it.

I will take another question. Is this not enlightening? [**Yes.**]
Samuel: Could I just follow up with what you said?

Yes, you may.

In terms of beingness—my understanding, though limited it may be, in beingness, there is no notion of value given to it being good or bad. Each reflects upon the other; each defines the other. And to that end, one cannot be without the other. And where beingness comes in is to see that totality, that functioning of the dualistic relationship necessary to have that experience.

So it gets back to the point of righteousness and what it really means to be a righteous person. You just said that it means to have a right relationship with the Father. And yet, the state of beingness is such that the concept of a [Heavenly] Father falls away. There's just oneself. There's just being. Am I making this overly complicated? Is there something that I am not getting that's so apparently obvious, here, in terms of a distinction? Because there seems to be some type of qualitative difference between good and evil, the light being preferred to the darkness, to strive for one versus the other where, in fact, from what I would understand as beingness, it's not wanting the light over the darkness, it's not preferring good to evil. It's just accepting that these things exist, for they are a manifestation of the dualistic reality of how we experience life.

Is he in trance? [**Laughter.**]

Who knows? It's a dream anyway, so I could be.

God Perceives His Reality

All of these are intellectual concepts. It's all left-brain. There are no words necessary to explain anything as you peer into the area where I come from. All is known by the mind and all is seen as one because they come from One mind and are truly one.

Understanding at this level is immediate and totally comprehensive. The mind sees; the mind knows; all questions gone! For this reason, at this level, we can see the manifestation of all as God's will, as taken from the world of God's thoughts. Yes, thoughts are energy and your world is a God-manifested thought form. But it is a play of his mind that he is enjoying even as you watch, consciously or unconsciously, the play of your own thoughts. Who is a dreamer but one who contemplates and enjoys his own thoughts. The inventors and creators of this world are both dreamers and doers. They dream their thoughts and then act to bring them into solid form. God is a dreamer and a doer!

To explain all this by some kind of intellectual process is a part of what's necessary in the life of duality. In other words, in order for all the people in this room to understand you, you had to put your thinking into words, correct? [**Yes.**] They cannot see your mind. But if we should go higher and higher into your mind, we would see the totality of your thinking and no words would be necessary. Ultra, advanced searching would lead us to the very presence of God flowing constantly as love and light in and through your mind. In God's presence all is known and no words are necessary. What is more, at this level of awareness you discern absolutely that all is one, there is no "other." And you come to understand that all creation is nothing more than God's thinking out loud. This is the ultra-state of human awareness when all duality disappears and silence and eternal peace fills and covers the soul.

So, yes, it is true, good and evil are just concepts. They are concepts created and manifested overtly as object lessons for man, to perceive through polarity, the reality of self. As we have said before, the eye cannot see itself. Therefore, there must be an object, in this case a mirror, or some other object through which the eye can perceive that it is seeing. An eye in a totally darkened room, cannot see; it is just being. That's all. It cannot function in a darkened room, even as an eye of a blind person is just being, is just there in the socket. It's just being.

That was God's state: just being. All light. And until he created something outside of himself, projected his thought out and solidified it into what we call the material world, he could not know himself. And so in doing such, he could see himself, he could perceive his reality. But he could slip back and forth between duality and non-duality. His existence in the primordial state is non-duality. Just being.

Samuel: Actually if I could follow up just one last thing?

Yes, you may.

These are very Vedic or Taoist principles. Is there a reason why these principles... well, what is it about India and the Far East that, from what we understand, cradled these type of concepts?

Civilization's Cradle

It's where God chose to begin. He had to start somewhere. But even this world is just a concept. We see the world differently than you do. We see it in different levels or vibrations. Your globe is round to you, and it is to us, too. But we can also see stratification of one group of people above or below another in terms of their evolution of understanding. The people of that particular area, the cradle of civilization, was where God decided to start. He had to start somewhere. And that's where he started.

Was it environment? Was it the weather? Was it the color of the skin? None of those had anything to do with it. It was his decision. Was it subjective? I do not know the answer to that question. But he had to start somewhere. And so that's where he decided to start.

Starting in a primitive way, that is, without all the background knowledge you have from television and radio and reading, he had to start with fundamentals, symbols. And out of that began the creation of altars and the offering up of objects that those whom he created could come to know their relationship with the one who created them. Primitive as it was, he did not see the offering of the form; he saw the hearts of the people in hunger to know themselves, and to understand their origins. And that's where they began.

Samuel: If I could continue with that concept of symbols...

You need not preface your words by anything; just speak. Because what we are concerned about here is not personality. We're concerned about what information will be garnered on these tapes that will help others who are also questioning, that are ready to understand what you are understanding. Please understand, my son, we welcome all questions. If we cannot answer them, we will tell you.

Okay.

But we want to answer all questions.

You were talking about symbols and how Heavenly Father started, in a very basic way, to bring up the level of [human] understanding. You also mentioned earlier about prehistory,

QUESTIONS & ANSWERS WITH SAINT GERMAIN

and that man, being very ancient, going back several hundred million years…

I said 380 million.

380 million. Yes. And so, we've been around a long time, collectively as a species. We've experienced many civilizations. And I'm wondering where we are right now, compared to where civilizations have been, spanning all those years, that is, prehistory. In other words, on a scale from 1 to 10, where would we rank right now compared to the complete history of mankind in terms of the level that they've reached spiritually, as a civilization? Are we still at number 1? Are we on the 5 level? Are we kind of nearing the apex of where we can be as a species? Since I'm assuming that we might have reached the level prior to where we are right now, there is so much further we can go.

God's Measurement of Man

Where you err is that you have made a very civil world without love. You have law, you have lawyers—too many lawyers—you have all kinds of legal writings, laws on the books, and people to enforce them. We cannot say that your civilization is a high civilization under these circumstances. Were that love ruled, as was the original intention, your civilization would not have to have these kinds of things. While this culture of America is rich in its technology and its understanding of law and intellect, it is very poor in its ability to love correctly.

This is not meant to be a gross generalization, for there are exceptions. Most of you are exceptions. However, God's measurement of man is by the heart, not by the head. Words are often shallow or hollow. And people like to hear themselves talk. What God is looking for is the son or daughter who loves him so much that perpetually, that son or daughter is seeking him above all. He is seeking someone who loves him—just loves him; not to see what he or she can get from him, but to be one with the Father. Jesus was a poor man but his love for God was so great that night and day, he sought and sought for God within himself. And he found him. That is how he became a master.

So it is with many of us who are called masters at the supreme level of spiritual development. As a civilization, of course, there's a greater amount of what we would call being "civilized" here than in the past. But I can tell you that primitive man, in many ways, was more civilized. Because while he didn't have all the intelligence and didn't have all the knowledge of outer space, he knew *inner* space. He knew God lived in him. There was little or nothing to distract him from that encounter. There was no television to watch; there were no baseball games to go to; there was no recreation like there is now. And so he was fortunate to be able to go inward.

You may think, "primitive" or "cave man"; I do not. I think of a man living in a cave who, due to his isolation, would draw more inwardly. Many did, and many became masters. Man is older than 380 million. I just quoted a recent figure. So God made provision, long before you ever came upon this earth, for there to be a truly civilized being, a civilized nation. They came and they went. Their foundations were based upon master teachers and highly evolved individuals who led them. But when those individuals were gone, the masses reverted back to their animal-like nature. But there had been, among all these civilizations, master teachers and guides who understood what

I have spoken about. They did not always call him "God," but they understood their own divinity. And they understood the source of that divinity was inside and beyond themselves.

In those early stages of humanity God had to intercede, even as you, as a parent, must explain pictorially and most clearly to your child, the things of life. And when you don't want a child to stick their fingers into something where they will burn themselves or be electrocuted, you have to show them and say, "Don't do this with this. Don't touch this stove. Don't touch this; this is hot."

So God, starting out with primitive man, had to be a part of man. He had to mingle with him and make himself very apparent. As they were his first children, his love for them was so great. His desire for the takeoff of man correctly was so passionate, so detailed, so well planned. And so many of them—*many* of them—knew that they were being guided by God, by spirits, by the angelic world. They saw, with open eyes, the presence of the spirit world. They did not have to sit [in meditation] to develop. They were born that way.

So primitive man may look "primitive," but his soul was often highly developed and filled with great love.

Does this lead you to a tributary question? [**Laughter.**]

Brianna: If we could go on—with just one brief question—with this concept of prehistoric civilizations, and very advanced civilizations. In modern times, this is referred to as an Atlantean type of civilization. It doesn't matter to me whether they actually existed or not, but my understanding would be that it correlates to just what you had said, in terms of somewhere back in the past there were civilizations that had reached a certain level of awareness, much higher than we are right now. Not necessarily technologically speaking, but heart-wise and spiritually. And for whatever reason, just over the course of history, they gave way to something new. That's all I wanted to say. But is that a fair assessment in terms of where that Atlantean notion, perhaps, might have come from? That myth that goes back into the ethers…

'Twas not a myth, my daughter.

Okay.

Ancient Civilizations

Such civilizations did exist. Let it be understood that most myths are based upon a truth. They simply look like a myth because people have added to them, but their core reality is true. Such civilizations did exist; they were highly advanced. It is not unlike the Roman Empire. If you go there, you will only see broken columns, and partial walls, broken off faces, parts of statues. But at its height, Rome was very modern. Running water. Public latrines and baths. Hot and cold running water, brought in from the mountains. Ice was available. They were highly civilized. Today you would never know all that, unless your archaeologists had done their diggings and findings.

These civilizations come and go, with the rise and fall of leaders and the people who follow them, who think that they (the leaders) are God. That is the danger in your own present civilization, your own present culture, here in America. Unless the leadership understands clearly that they are under the guidance of God, and not God himself, then they, too, can meet with such a fate. Whoever gave anyone the right—anywhere—even against the 10 commandments, to take another person's life? And yet, it is done wholesale. But since it is all an illusion, we need not worry, correct? [**Yes.**] Yes.

Lynn: Saint Germain, is it correct to aspire toward a time when all of humanity will experience this advanced level of spiritual understanding, and live in harmony and peace? Or is that really never destined to happen? In other words, individuals will make that advancement during the course of struggling with, you know, lesser advancement, etc., etc. Can there be a time when everyone will be enlightened?

The Dream of God

That is man's dream, isn't it? [**Yes.**] The Kingdom of Heaven on Earth. Paradise. It is a dream found prolifically throughout humanity. But if that happens, the dream will be over.

"Game over."

That will mean everyone will have gone home. And so, it's in the hands of God, the creator and the destroyer, to determine if he wants to wake up or not. And if he does, in his cosmic mind—where all of this is being played out—the dream will be over. Mind you, you are now in God's mind. Right now.

You are a dream. You are an object in God's mind; just energy formed by God. I repeat, you are in his mind. If he chooses to wake up, you're done with. You're gone.

But we do not see that happening. God is enjoying the game. He is enjoying learning about himself in his multifaceted reality. By creating more beings, and through the expansion of the population, he knows more of himself. So we do not see that likelihood. Nor do we see the likelihood of a kingdom of heaven on earth. There are civilizations like the one you are in now, which are more civilized in many ways in the outer aspects—though I take exceptions on the *inner* aspects—where you have established a *kind* of kingdom of heaven on earth. But it's a false heaven, not a lasting heaven.

Once you reach that place of fully awakening to God living within you and yourself as God, and you enjoy that great unending joy; it will be with you always. It will never, never, never leave you. Once you are awakened fully, then heaven is for you on earth. How many will do that? That depends, is it in their script? Are they ready? Have they evolved enough? And so on and so on.

Jewel: Saint Germain, I'm listening to what you are saying, and I'm finding myself confused about the concept of free will. How does that play in each of our lifetimes? When it seems sometimes you're saying, that we are all just playing a certain role in this dream?

The Tapestry of God's Dream

Yes, easily answered. This question was answered in a prior question and answer session with Saint Germain. The bird out here on the limb appears to have freedom. Freedom of will. That it can will itself to go anywhere. Not true. Its instinct, that is, the built-in mechanism called instinct, has confined it to a certain pattern of flight; it stays within a territory and does not go outside of it. It can only build its nest in a certain way. And it flies about within the circumference of that designated territory. Within that, it looks very spontaneous and as if it has free will, and it does.

So, too, human beings have, within divine law, a prescribed territory of freedom. But you do not have the freedom to kill yourself. You may, but that is not what we call "free will." That's taking advantage of your freedom. But if it's in your script, you will do it anyway. You will go against free will.

But God did not want you to feel like a robot. That is another way of saying that *he* did not want to feel like a robot. Nor would it feel as if it was a real game if he put parameters around it, "Thou shalt only do what thou art told." Rather, he works through your own conscience, and guides you.

You may be driving along only to have a subtle experience in your mind that you must go back home—that there's something seriously wrong. And so you drive back, and sure enough, you find that you left the tea kettle on the burner, and it is boiled out, and about to burn. Spirit alarmed you of the impending problem at home. Yes, your memory is a part of it, which we in spirit access to protect and guide you (in this case, with the tea kettle). In this hypothetical situation, because it is in your script, we were able to warn you.

In some other cases, it is not in the script to be warned, and the tea kettle burns and the whole house burns down. Who decided either outcome? I pose this question to cause you to think about whether you really have free will or not.

What appears as freedom is within a prescribed area and prescribed actions. But overall, the thread of your life is being woven into the tapestry of God's dream, and is held in the hand of God. He knows where it flows in and flows out; how it is to fit into the total pattern of the tapestry, that he can complete it.

Jewel: I need to ask if we can change anything? I mean, how do we? How are we able to change and grow…

Waking Up from the Dream

My dear one, not everyone awakens to the fact that they need to change and grow. If it is in your script to think that, it will be played out and you will do so. That is the grace of God.

God's love descends in the form of grace. There are times when it appears as if he has superceded his plan. There is no such a thing as superceding his plan. It is all a part of the game, you see. With the little red toy soldier you hold in your hand, you read the instructions to the game which say that you are supposed to go after all the little toy soldiers in the black uniform. It is the same when you play any of your other games, like Monopoly. The games come with instructions. To play the game you read and follow those directions. If your instructions tell you that you have freedom to do so and so, and you do it, then that means it's in your script and allowance has been made.

I know that it makes it appear as if you have absolutely no freedom. But you have to remember that you are God playing a game. And that your duty, your responsibility, is to wake up and go home, not to keep playing the game. You won't stop before it's time, but you will, when it is your time.

Did we answer your question?

Jewel: I think I just need to integrate it a bit.

The Game of Life

What did we say to you through this medium last week? "Watch yourself. [**Yes.**] Watch life. [**Yes, you did.**] Watch how you create your own reality. Watch how you respond to things around you."

As time goes by, you will understand who you are. Who you *really* are. And you will understand that you're more than what you appear to be. That you're outside of all of this, just watching it unfold. That is the beginning, you see, of awakening. [**Yes.**] When the child on the floor is playing with his friend, and says, "Hey, this is only a game. I don't have to take it so seriously," the game is almost over, you see? [**Yes.**]

So we want to bring you—not to disturb you or to mess up your life, so to speak—to that place of awakening whereby you begin to say, "Hey, this is just a game," then you are close to that place where the game is almost over. You want to do it in this lifetime, do you not? [**Yes!**]

This is a follow up. This is Jim, Saint Germain.

Yes.

Jewel was speaking about free will and it seems as life proceeds for the whole world, our choices increase, in terms of what we can do. I guess what I struggle with some-times—not sometimes, a *lot*—is making those choices, when you're just not sure which way to go.

I mean, you want to do the will of God, but you're not really sure what that is. And it's not like you're also choosing good or evil—there are just [every day life] choices. And when you're making those choices, you obviously want to do the will of God. I know that; we've listened, at times, to tapes channeled by Abraham.

I know of Abraham, yes.

Abraham instructs you to go with your gut, and with feel-ing. That when you do those things, and then things don't turn out exactly as you would imagine them to be, you start wondering, "Did I choose wrongly?" And so I'm wondering, is Abraham correct in that? Could you help us with that?

Living Your Dharma

Again, keep this in mind in life. Just keep it as a sign in front of you. Write it indelibly on your forehead: "I am on this path, I am in this life in order to learn about myself and wake up." And so choice is not about if you walk into the woods and your gut feeling is go to the left, and you find out that leads you in the direction away from where you need to go, and since you're not finding your way out of the woods, you then turn to the right, and walk straight ahead 50 feet, and again you make a decision. If your gut feeling is to go this or that way, and you make a mistake—you are learning about you. Being in the woods is only a symbol. It's only an opportunity for you to learn about you, on whatever level that you discern.

God, the Father, is always a parent. Not "apparent," but always being *a parent* with you. He's always guiding you, either directly interiorly with you in your consciousness, and/or with we master teachers and guides outside of you. We coordinate together. We understand this process. You will be guided to conclude what you're to conclude. That's why we say, do whatever you do, and do not worry about the outcome. When you have an idea that things should turn out thus and so, according to the way that you turned or the decision you made, that's when you err. You have to look at the outcome and say, "What am I supposed to learn from this?"

For example, being in business, as you are, you've made certain decisions, and sometimes the outcome was not always to your liking. Did you quit?

No.

Why did you not stop?

Because I believe in the dream.

You believe in the dream, but also what did you get from that mistake, or that wrong step, or the fact that it did not yield what you wanted? What did you learn?

I learned lessons.

Did you learn the lesson of external reality, or internal reality?

Both.

Both, yes. Because both are necessary. The environment is created by God, and the internal reality of who you are is God. So they are coordinated. But one is given that the other may be known. God created all of the universe, not so that in the end he could worship the universe, but so he could learn about himself.

The journey is not about what you're doing *on* the journey, although again, we say, whenever you take up any project, large or small, act as if everything depended on you and pray as if everything depended upon God.

Why? Because you must do your *dharma*. That is, you must do the thing that you were called to do with all of your heart, mind and soul, to find yourself. If you don't do it with all your heart, mind and soul, you will not live the adventure which will lead you into all the circumstances to teach you about you. Those individuals who are not courageous enough to take up an adventure to step out and do what they are called to do, will never learn about their higher and deeper self.

Many people awaken to God in the center of tragedy. Many people have been imprisoned, even in a military prison camp, and were visited by an angel. When their circumstances were so desperate, and they become so hungry searching, this brought about their quick awakening. So all the circumstances of your life are there to teach you about you. In other words, you are God, learning about God, that you may wake up and go home.

Again, the more you step outside of yourself, to look at your so-called reality and this illusion, the more you will wake up, the less will you be undone. The less will you be concerned about outcome, and you will say that under all circumstances, "Father, you are leading me to the correct end. I am coming home." You will accept all things on your path, and know they are the will of God.

Lynn: Saint Germain, on behalf of people who may read this material in the future, one common question might be, are we the only civilization in the material world, on this planet, or are there other planets, galaxies, systems, universes, where there exists a material manifestation? Is mankind, as we know it, all there is at this time, or are there other civilizations struggling for their enlightenment as well?

Mysteries Revealed?

I will say to you, without being too evasive, that when you have reached the place with God that you need to be, then you will know the answer to that question. Until that time, you need to focus upon your own arrival to God. Otherwise, it is just intellectual curiosity which would take you outside the realm of your needing to know.

This is not a chastisement. It is, again, the effort here, with what we are doing, to enable you to focus. Most of the answers of life—well, I should say, *all* the answers to life—are in God. Once you reach him, you can ask him yourself. Not only ask in the sense of verbalizing, but you will see as you peer into that Ocean of Light, "Hey, there are other civilizations, there are other beings. So he *did* think beyond Mother Earth." *Or,* "He didn't." (I threw that in so that the mystery may remain a mystery!)

Annie: Yes, Saint Germain—This is Annie. What is the best way to get rid of fear? I started realizing that when I did a spiritual reading for someone or gave advice from an intuitive level, I would experience an inner conflict.

Could you explain what you mean by conflict? Are we talking about hearing your authentic voice and then hearing a contradictory commentary? [**Yes.**] And what is the fear?

The fear comes from saying one thing that I believe to be the truth and then experiencing that that might not be the right answer but another that is in my mind could be the right answer. It is like having two voices in my head. So I become torn.

And can you give us an example here?

For example, when I gave Jewel a spiritual reading in class the other night. I told her what I saw but then doubted it.

I thought that I may have misinterpreted what I saw in my mind. Ever since that reading, I started having a fear.

That you spoke something incorrectly? [**Yes.**]

Bridging the Two Worlds

Yes. It has been the same with this medium, as it has been with many mediums when they first start out doing this precious work. In the beginning it is sometimes like stepping into a mine field. You don't know exactly where it is safe to step. But you dare to step anyway.

As Philip has said to you in the past, you have to be willing to make a fool of yourself. If your motivation was to somehow deceive Jewel, as you spoke of your conflict a few moments ago, then you should have some uncomfortable feeling. That means your soul was not in the proper place. But if, in fact, you erred accidentally, or you had some oversight, or you realized something later, there is no concern for fear. You have done your best. You can't do better than that. You can even go back to the person and tell them that upon closer scrutiny you found something else or some additional information.

Don't strive for perfection in this work in the sense that you can never be wrong. Otherwise, with ego in the way, you may alter the content of what we in the spirit world actually want to convey through you to others. If you are a "true" medium, you are not in charge anyway. By the very definition of the word "medium" you are simply a means— a conveyor—of truth that we stream through you. If you are doing otherwise, you are not a true medium. To do this work effectively, you have to get out of the way and let us do, through you, what we need to do for the good of the person receiving our message.

This is why we told Philip years ago that he must train to do the highest and best work, which includes learning how *not* to be involved from an ego level, as to what comes through him. If the medium is thoroughly trained, objective, and of a highly moral character, that is all he can do. If this is so, then he is of highest use to us and is a true bridge between your world and our world. As a truly objective instrument in our hands, given all the right circumstances, he cannot be responsible. Again, as a true medium, how can he be responsible; he's just a channel. It is the receiver who must be responsible for what he or she receives.

Is the hose that the water comes through responsible for the water? No, it is only a conductor, a passageway. Then as the individual receives the water, what they do with that water, whether they drink it, they wash with it, they bathe their eyes in it, bathe their child, water a plant, is up to them. They become responsible for the information, or the "water" that comes through. Have I made myself clear? [**Yes.**] So get beyond the sense of fear.

We who come from fundamental backgrounds sometimes try to balance things in a very black and white way. That this is right and this is wrong. There are shades of gray in between. I would say we have to get beyond that kind of thinking to understand God is not standing by with a whip when you fail, to hit you. Or just to embrace you when you make everything correct. God loves you under all circumstances. Put fear aside.

That which you were giving to Jewel was in this class and was only practice. You were doing your best to be a good conveyor of the truth as you discerned it. It was only your effort to be a good channel. And being a purest you feared failure or having misled someone. What this shows to us on this side is that you are a very pure soul.

This same kind of thing happened to Philip. From childhood he was paralyzed many times in fear that he had made a mistake. His fear was sometimes so great that it would paralyze him for days. That is because he had a pure mind. He did not want to disappoint God or be a failure.

When such a state of mind is to the extreme, it becomes a kind of neurosis. Individuals who have neuroses can't be good mediums. This does not mean that you can just say anything about anything; you have to be attuned. The process of being attuned is accomplished through proper meditation.

I have a question, Saint Germain. This is John.

Yes, John.

This has to do with my reality and my efforts to master myself. When I read the book you channeled through Philip, *To Master Self is to Master Life,* I very much resonated with its contents. If I cannot accomplish self-mastery in this life time, can I do it in the spirit world or do I have to keep coming back?

The Core of Self-Mastery

There are many chances. I did not say that growth was not possible in the spirit world; it's just much harder. This physical body and the spirit work together for that growth. That was God's intention, which is what I said this morning, if you remember. But my admonition to everyone is: the more you forget yourself—this is going to be a paradox, because on one hand we say, "in order to help others, you need to help yourself"—but to find self, you have to lose yourself.

To lose yourself, you have to be involved in concern for others. It does not mean masses of people, though you may pray for masses; at least get outside of yourself. For there, in that action, you can find yourself more clearly and truly achieve self-mastery. Because self-mastery, at its core, is the mastery of directing love. Unconditional love.

When you have achieved the ability to love all people as yourself—regardless of what they do or do not do, regardless of who they are, where they are, what age, what time—you have achieved self mastery. That's the pinnacle of self-mastery. So the key to self-mastery is getting outside of self. Being aware of self, yes, making sure that self is being nurtured correctly, yes. But in the end, after you've done all that, you must give out.

The purpose of a fruit tree is not just to send its root into the ground, that it may stabilize and feed itself; it is to bear fruit that others may pick from it. That is its giving out. So it sends its roots deeply into the soil; it feeds itself, it expands under the presence of the elements, the air, the water, the sunshine, and then it bears fruit which it gives out. A fruit tree, by its very name, has its greatest value not just as a shade tree, but in giving out fruit. And it reaches the fulfillment of what it was created for, or perfection, self-mastery, by bearing fruit for others.

I am very touched at this moment by what I have just said, because I have spoken this truth so many times. I hope you get it. [**Yes.**] It means so much to me, as I am speaking it, because it is what I live for: to see you bear true spiritual fruit for self and others, and thus in this way, master your own self.

Ninety-nine percent of the world's problems would be eliminated if each one would reach out to others and help them. Then the neuroses, the anger, the selfishness, the lust, the greed would all be dispelled. They are not the cause of your problem. Those are resultant from being separated from your ideal self, or God.

When you truly come into the midst of God's love, all those lesser things fall away. They have no place to grow or be. So many have it backwards, fighting the devil, when they should be using that same energy to find God within.

We have spoken enough for today. I shall take my leave with the warmest of memories of this time.

God bless you, this is Saint Germain.   (III)

This is Todd. Saint Germain, what happens to someone who is buried without a formal or religious ceremony?

Ceremony, or no ceremony, God's love emanates to all. The manmade rules and regulations often have nothing to do with the ultimate reality of what happens to a soul. Because an individual is known by God, and therefore loved by God, that individual is taken care of when he comes to our side. Ritual is ritual and often doesn't have anything to do with any requirement set down by God. But the fact of that soul is *fact!* There are those over whom all kinds of laudatory things have been said at their funerals, when in actuality they were scoundrels, and vice versa.

The funeral service and burial does not make the person. The person's own life makes the person, and the condition *after* life is determined by the content of his soul. It is as black and white as a newspaper. That is the criteria by which to judge what happens to an individual with or without a burial ceremony.

God bless you. This is Saint Germain.   (IV)

Sylvia: Does it make any difference to Providence whether our body is buried or cremated?

Burial versus Cremation

No, it makes no difference, because "you" are not there anyway. In fact, it can be more harmful for you in "leaving your body" to worry about the disposal of it, than to center upon the more vital concern of moving into the spirit world. What is more, concern about your body may draw you back to the earth plane. Such worry can become obsessive in nature. That is why graveyards are "haunted." That's why homes are "haunted," to use your earthly vernacular.

Rather, be indifferent as to what happens to your body. Designate, if you want, either by word of mouth or by will, how you want it disposed of. But it does not really matter because you are not the body, any more than the caterpillar is not the butterfly.

This is Brian. Since we are all a part of God, is it necessary to bring the people who have murdered young children to justice?

God's Spiritual Justice

The universe is run by laws that maintain equanimity, that keep the balance of things. Even your own body is maintained by these same laws. It repels water when you bathe, lest you drown. In the same way, when one goes against the laws of either physical nature or moral law there is retribution. Not always immediately, but eventually there is a price to pay for unlawful action. This is true of your mind as much as of your body. As the body would reject a foreign object that might harm it, so society rejects those who have done wrong to the body of mankind.

It is the law working which is equitable. However, what is "wrong" in the world today is how we treat such individuals. Imprisonment may be necessary to isolate such an individual, even as the harmful microbe in the body needs to be isolated from the rest of the cells to keep it from harming the whole. However, earthly prison systems are not about reform, they are about isolation and punishment. There is no way a person in such circumstances can change without ample education and a proper environment in which to live.

Education, from God's point of view, is about bringing forth self-knowledge and amplifying the light within and increasing awareness of the same. In this arena, your prison system has failed miserably.

There is great work that needs to be done in the earthly penal system. There is a mission for someone and many. There is standing waiting a great multitude of imprisoned people—both behind physical bars and those that are behind mental bars—who need to be enlightened about the facts of who they really are interiorly. In essence, they are all divine and made of light.

Catherine: Do you have anything to say about the political climate in America today?

The True Nature of Governing

We spoke earlier that it is not what happens in life that is important. It is how we *respond* to it. Life is comprised of sowing and reaping. It is the same in every area of life, including politically. Therefore, we must be very careful what we do with our life energies lest they come back to us in some detrimental way. It is no different in the political world, you see. We see from our side that too often decisions are made in government that, while well meaning, have little or nothing to do with God or the rightness of things. Rather, often it is *not* the truth of things that counts but the effort to be in power at any price. Your earthly laws are not the laws of heaven. In many cases they are manmade, having little or nothing to do with true justice.

If, in fact, true love reigned in society, government would not be necessary in the structured way in which it exists, for each person would govern himself correctly, society would move or exist together harmoniously, and all things would work together for the purpose of the whole and for the good of the individual. From our perspective, for the progression of humanity, we may intercede to try to cause a certain thing to happen because we see adverse circumstances if another path is taken.

Certainly, what is happening in America's governmental culture is not the only and greatest problem. The greater problem and the root of all your earthly and spiritual problems is resultant from what is seen as "self." As long as you identify with this earth and your present body as "self," you cannot awaken to the eternal you! Even the president of your country or any leader of any country could affect the future of that country eternally by dwelling upon the reality of God as primary and create an enlightened nation. This "self" I speak of can only be known through higher realization. And in that realization there would be the dawning of the fact that God is, that he is not out there somewhere, as many religions teach, but has his being *in each of us!* What a different world this would be if all were enlightened to this level of "self." How differently would leaders lead if all knew what I say to be fact and not a matter of faith. We are leading earth to this eventual realization so that governments of the distant future may govern righteously.

When that awareness of "self" dawns and divinity is understood worldwide, will it not be a different world? Could you harm another if you understood that they were from the same source as you? That you are, in fact, from the same parent, and you are brothers and sisters? And that each one of you is a light being and divine?

Because man is ignorant to the essential truth of life—blind to the spiritual world, blind to the purpose of life—there are many things which imitate life or are false. Under such circumstances, we can only encourage the dawning of the light within those who are ready to awaken to it. It is they who will change culture ultimately, but in the end, every individual—from the least to the greatest—must face this truth of self, whomever they may be, and live accordingly—if not in this world, then the next.

Life is not about these outer activities. These are man-made. Life is about what kind of person one can ultimately become—through all of their life experiences—and about being a truly good person.

Saint Germain, thank you for your words. This is Patricia. I have been working with a teaching that has to do with channeling earth energy to the body. Through experimentation with these teachings I have come to understand about a higher self and a lower self. I have been trying to observe what that is, and how I have, through my childhood experiences, come to kind of create my personality, in having different experiences or wounds happen to me in my life. The premise of the work is to discover the wound and the defenses I have put up resultantly. I was wondering if you have any opinion about this particular teaching?

Healing Energies

You have a beautiful blue aura, indicative of your soul evolution and the spiritual force that is working with you. I say that to encourage you, not to flatter you.

I don't have an opinion. In the spirit world there are no "opinions" from whence I come, there is only truth. "Opinion" is an individual view of phenomenon. Where I come from we all know the true view of all things.

You are working with healing energies. It is all one energy. As regards the journey to God through this path, there is truth to it. The path, the drama unfolding in your life, is there for a purpose. Not all comes from the intervention of low spirits or evil spirits. Some things are allowed to happen because they are to teach us. Some of the worst events and some of the most devastating experiences that have happened to individuals have resultantly made the greatest souls.

Again, those who look at life constructively are those who can turn a thing of sorrow into a thing of joy, a thing of difficulty into victory. The major thing is this: there are many, many misconceptions about life. Why do you think that, in spite of all of the spiritual teachings and all the good people who have come on earth, we do not yet have "heaven on earth"? Because there is yet much ignorance, even in religion. Much of religion is manmade. Manmade views! Some of them are very good. Parts of them serve the ends of men—individually and collectively.

However, the earthly mind is woven of misconceptions as well as truths. So to get to the real mind—that is, the divine mind, which lies hidden beneath this composite of truth and falsehood—one must go through struggles and overcome them. In that sense, psychology and therapy are good, to the degree that they help remove ignorance and relieve pain. Ultimately though, any spiritual teaching, to be a true teaching, must go beyond just relieving pain. It must eventually lead the person to the experience of his own being, which is to know that he or she is divine and all that is happening outwardly is to teach and lead them to this fact.

So many are looking *outward* into the darkness, and wondering why they cannot see the path. They cannot see the true path because they looking in the wrong direction. The true path leads *inward*—to the light within their soul—and also to the Source of all Light. As you ponder what I say, my words will be a comfort and give you proper direction in your search for self. Ultimately, you will find great peace and liberation will come to your soul. Please work—all of you—to realize this before you die.   (V)

Saint Germain, this is Rebecca. My question is: of all the churches, which are the nearest to what God desires?

The True Religion

Beloved one, your question is a very important one, but when we talk about churches, what we are really talking about is the Christian religion. The "church" is merely an outer form through which the Christian religion is taught and institutionalized.

The *true* religion is the religion of love. There really is only one religion, and it is the religion of love. At the highest level of the spirit world there are no churches—there is only love. Church is a manmade tool. Church consists of a body of believers who come together to express their individual and combined worship of God. Therefore, man's establishment of the church was a convenience, a place for people to gather to draw closer to God in fellowship.

But where does the real "church" exist? It exists in you. You are the living church. God is not interested in dead churches. God is not interested in people gathering and simply giving lip service through ritual to him, either in the burning of candles or the singing of songs. These rituals are very external. For if we do them, yet are empty and do not seek and long for him—the Author of Life—then those experiences can be very empty, indeed. This you have already experienced.

In these latter years of your life, wherever you may find the greatest comfort and meaning, that is the best church for you. But my admonition to you is to dwell upon the fact that almighty God—as powerful as he is—has his place of dwelling in you. *You* are the "church."

The Role of the Conscience

Jesus himself said indirectly that man was the temple of God, therefore, when God is seeking to guide us, each one perceives—to varying degrees—that he is speaking to us through us. That's what conscience is. When we live a life that is moral, then the conscience becomes the clear voice of God. When we live an immoral life, then God, through our conscience, still guides us but we do not hear him as clearly. But for those who live morally, the conscience is very clear and it speaks very loudly. That is God speaking through us to us.

Therefore, your question is most important regarding your ultimate entrance into the eternal, spirit world. The best way to prepare for that is to follow the *religion of love.* This means, love everyone, unconditionally. Love individuals as you love yourself; treat them as you would treat yourself. In the practice of that kind of love you become the favorite place for Heavenly Father to dwell most fully.

Celebrating Your Own Divinity

You cannot come to the spiritual world and find God here unless you find God on earth, in *yourself.* If you find him in yourself, speak to him and celebrate your own divinity—the center of which is him—when you come here, immediately your heart will know that God lives in you. And you will see him in everyone and in everything.

Practice that on earth now. When you look at a flower, you already do this. But now do it on a deeper level. When you look at a flower, try to see God's genius in it—God's beauty, the truth of God, God's love—in its color, its shape, its texture, its fragrance. When you look at a dog or even a bug, a rock or crow or another human being, look for God. Look for God in each one of them. If you will practice that for the balance of your life, then gradually the *blindness* regarding God's existence as being in everything, everywhere will disappear. And in your latter years you will begin to "see" more and more fully the reality of God's presence in everything, everywhere, at all times! That is the most important thing.

But first, see God in yourself. It begins with gratitude. Gratitude for life. Gratitude for all blessings. And then take the time to commune. Not just to ask him for things. Not just to talk to him in times of need. But truly—as you sit on the porch swing or anywhere and in your mind—hold his hand and allow him to hold yours. Let him come and embrace you and show you his love. His is a love that transcends physical love, that transcends human love. Let him pour over you and through you with love. Let him emanate *from* you to others.

Jesus tried to teach this reality when he said, "I am in the Father, and the Father is in me. He who has seen me has seen the Father." He also said, "If you do as I ask of you, I will no longer call you my servants, but my friends." He spoke of a state of equality, meaning that that which he was, you can become. So, if in your mind Jesus is the best example, follow and imitate him.

In any case, God is not restricted by man's concept of him. God can be whatever he wants to be and anywhere at any time that he needs to be, in order to lead one of his children home. In other words, he may be a rock. He may be the music on the radio speaking. He may be the silent voice in the heart. He may be something that you read in a newspaper. God will use every facet of life to reflect himself to us, to show himself to us, and make his presence known. Expand your thinking in this way, realizing again that you are the "church," and that the most important "church" is you.

Among the earth's religions, all are important. For the essential teaching of all religions is to seek and practice goodness, and to love others as much or more than your-self. If we live that way, then all religions have value. In the spiritual world you will find, however, that at the highest levels, it is the "religion" of love that has meaning. Churches exist [in the spiritual world] in lesser realms, because people in those lesser realms of spirit have not the awareness that the true church is the love of God, and that each being is the "church."

As I mentioned in the beginning, there are no churches in the higher realms. There is only the love of God. There are temples and manifestations and symbols and all kinds of things that reflect that. All of nature there reflects God—the energy, the music, the light, the color, the vibration.

I hope I have answered your question. I have tried to give a comprehensive answer because there is no simple one, except to say that each man or woman is the true church of God, the true temple of God, when he or she is fully focused on God and seeks and lives in that oneness.

I am sure my commentary has helped you. Contemplate what I have said and you will gain the insight needed to be a living church of God!

God bless you. This is Saint Germain.   **(VI)**

["Oh Holy Night" As the music fades out Saint Germain comes in...]

I am here. Good evening. This is Saint Germain.

I am so pleased that you could be here this evening, not only with me, but with the many, many gathered teachers and loved ones who have come here tonight in spirit to surround you. These occasions are planned on our side far in advance. Each soul on earth is brought to such an occasion according to divine will. It is your destiny to be here. Whatever it is that you gain tonight from this experience is what you are meant to gain.

My admonition is to be like a child because it is in this energy, this innocence, that Spirit does not only speak to you as I am speaking tonight through Philip, but in your innocence, Spirit will speak to you at *all* times. That is why it is said that unless you become as a little child, you shall not enter the Kingdom of Heaven.

I am not going to give a talk tonight. There have been many, many talks given for this [Christmas] season. Rather I come to salute the Christ in you. It is for that reason that Jesus came; he came to point the way to God within you.

So beloved ones, because you have needs, my gift to you for Christmas is to answer your questions as best I can. This holy hour will be comprised of your questions and my answers.

For those of you who have never met me, let me just say that I am like you. I aspire toward spiritual perfection and I sought to master the means by which to be used by God. So I am here under the auspices of that kind of energy, motivation, and endeavor.

Without saying more I would like to take the first question.

Robert: Saint Germain will you speak about the Maltese Cross?

What would you like to know about the Maltese Cross?

I have read that the cross signifies the heaven coming down, as the vertical, and the earth as the horizontal. I want to know how it came about and what it should signify? Is there more to it than that?

The Meaning of the Maltese Cross

The cross pre-existed Jesus. The cross is always, on the deepest level, the manifestation or the convergence of the vertical and the horizontal—the heavenly and the earthly. Or the mind and the body. Before you can achieve spiritual maturation you have to bring these two together by sacrificing ego. The cross has many, many meanings, but fundamentally spiritually, metaphysically this the basic meaning.

The Maltese Cross is but another of those manifestations from a different sphere of culture and society which had different meanings for those who used it, but fundamentally it represents spiritual attainment through sacrifice.

Paul: This is a little bit of a heady question… in history there have been many definitions about the good-evil conflict, from battles against Satan, to the yin and yang balance, to the harmony in Buddhism. On our path of self-realization there is an emphasis in literature on integration of the self, like one's weaknesses and strengths. But often when viewing self we define ourselves in terms of this good and evil. What I would like to know is: how does one resolve this duality and how should we view this dynamic?

Put the Shadow Behind You

Your question is an excellent question and very deep. Indeed, people around the world are in a quandary regarding this question. First of all, all achievement is interior—ultimately. It is the mastery of thought in achieving all goodness which motivates you to act and to speak of only good. Therefore, the initial goal of overcoming what you call "evil" is to achieve a clear understanding of the standard of goodness. It does not take much to know that because it is based upon divine love, unconditional love.

It is in doing goodness that you achieve your Christ-self. No one or nothing can touch you if, indeed, your thoughts are aligned with God. But often many people who believe in good and evil spend a great portion of their time fearing and fighting evil. In doing so they may deplete their positive energies. Secondly, they place the emphasis in the wrong place.

We who have achieved self-mastery understand that "yes," there are those individuals, as you can see them walking the face of the earth, who seek to do harm to others. Your prisons are filled with such individuals. And "yes," in the spirit world there are individuals in the lower spheres, whom we have seen with our own eyes, whose essential character is one of wishing ill and wanting to do harm to others. Most of this is based upon anger and jealousy—jealousy of what others have. Anger, because they do not have it, also.

But I would caution you, as I have been cautioned by my teachers: do not give any weight to evil. Put all of your energies into loving God, into knowing God. If you stand toward God, the source of all light, you have put the shadow behind you and it should remain behind you.

What did Jesus say? "Get behind me Satan!" That is where darkness should be and stay—thus you give no power to it. By resisting it, you draw it to you and give more power to it than is due.

The closer you get to God, the greater the light in you and all around you. It is a science. Ultimately, when you are 100% one with God, there is no shadow. How can there be when all is light?

Do not dwell on evil! When you seek to raise yourself up, do not spend time upon confession and guilt. What changes your life is change. And what is change but new action. When you draw upon the lesser things, the darkness, you draw it to you magnetically and it comes to dwell with you.

For example, let us say that during your childhood someone called you some unsavory names; if you, in turn, sought to defend yourself or get back at them, then they achieved their goal. They got your attention and they got you upset and engaged in their kind of negative energy. Whereas if you had just ignored the taunting, not even giving it one ounce of attention, then that individual would have been discouraged and gone away.

The lower spirits, the diabolical and harmful spirits, can by no means invade you if there is no basis for invasion. So don't create one by thinking that if you resist them you are doing good either for yourself or God. Turn away. Turn away!

When the doctor is operating on a tumor in the body, he does not spend his time at the operating table paying undue attention to the tumor after it is removed. He places it in a pan to be taken to the lab. He then gets on with bringing the operation to closure and sending the patient on his way within a now healthy body.

Have I made my answer clear? It is vitally important that you learn this because in the higher levels of spirit world we do not talk about evil. We know it is there, but we have no reason to talk about it. We have risen above it, and we want nothing to do with it. We will help those who are fighting evil on lesser levels, and we will help those who *want* to help others, but we who have risen above do not participate in that type of thing. Rather, we have won our freedom from it.

Saint Germain, this is Don.

Good evening, Don.

Saint Germain, could you speak to us for a moment about the institution of marriage and the concept of spiritual marriage as written about by Yogananda and others, as well as your ideas on how two people can form the most perfect union? Thank you.

Ultimate Marriage

I wish I had about three days to answer your question. [From a female member of the audience was heard, "We can sleep over!" To which Saint Germain humorously replied, "I cannot!" The audience broke into gales of laughter.]

In any case, all of you here spiritually sat forward on your seat when he asked this question about marriage. It is because all of you are either contemplating it, or have been through it, or are *through* with it. [Again, the audience broke into laughter.]

You came into this world as a single individual and you will leave this world as a single individual. Love, being the compelling principle, will determine whether you shall again be together with the one whom you have loved on earth.

Ultimate marriage is the marriage between God and you as an individual. If *that* marriage does not take place, then marriage between a husband and wife may consequently suffer. It is important to understand that if you chose to marry, then you are choosing consciously to take a path of the highest earthly calling and the possibility of the most fulfilling love of your life.

When experienced at the highest possible level, it is a love that partakes of the love of God. At the very least, it can imitate God's love, which is unconditional. Planned by God as the supreme path to self-knowledge, it can be, therefore, the most challenging experience in love and, when achieved, the most fulfilling.

When one is truly successful in marital love, such love yields the greatest joy, the highest fulfillment physically and spiritually and the ultimate experience of heaven on earth. It becomes a spiritual marriage when God is consciously included as dwelling in each, and honored as such in a transcendent love. Then you have a marriage in heaven as well as on earth. And that marriage may continue into eternity.

There are many, many obstacles on the path of marriage. You know that in order to achieve perfect oneness, you must put aside ego. You must see your couple from afar. You recognize that each of you shares and overlaps your responsibilities and does not expect one to carry the weight over the other. That is a great aspect of the "ideal" marriage.

However, you are not speaking of ideal marriage; you are speaking of marriage as it is. So to achieve that higher state that I speak of as being ideal, you have to pass through and surmount your struggles.

When you have difficulties in your marriage, as many people are having today, do not take it as if your marriage is with the wrong mate. Rather, keep working on your relationship. Unless you have tried and tried and tried, you cannot say that you have sought to make a successful marriage.

If all else fails, then you may consider that this was only a passing relationship or a "mistake" from which the two of you derived what you were to derive and it is now time to move on. However, we find in the scheme of God's creation that there are no mistakes, only the opportunity to learn and grow.

Rather, when you are tested ask yourself, "What is it that *I* am not doing correctly?" Don't place the responsibility on your mate. If each one will do this in the relationship, the things you are to learn, you will learn. Marriage is not about changing the other. It is about the most intimate, compassionate and passionate love and having the blessing of such love changing you.

Many couples do not talk to each other on the deeper things of life. Somehow, in their naïveté, they think when they marry, because of the love glow that was upon the relationship prior to marriage, that this glow will last. God created it that way so that marriage could *begin*. [**Laughter.**] Without it, many would not marry, because you are not attracted to someone unless there is something which causes you to be attracted. That is the law. But as you raise your love up, through sacrificial, unconditional love toward each other, then each soul will grow.

The Marriage Foundation

Again I say, many couples do not communicate. By communication, I do not mean yelling and screaming. I do not mean demanding verbally or by using body language to indicate how you think that they [your mate] *should* be.

You cannot change them. You cannot cause them to be anything. You can only change yourself. You can only cause yourself to be what *you* need to be. But if you will learn to communicate, in mutual respect for the other's thoughts and feelings, seen in the most objective manner, to discuss the various problems, questions, difficulties and struggles—and do this regularly—many, many marriages, thought to be doomed, would be saved.

Is there an ideal marriage? Is there a God? The answer is the same. Yes, there is a God. Yes, there is ideal marriage. But an ideal marriage, as far as we can discern and experience it, must consciously include God.

Is marriage ultimately necessary? Yes and no. You have masculinity and femininity within yourself. It is the "marriage" of these two, centered upon divine love, that ultimately brings you into complete consummation of your relationship with God. In the truly spiritually arrived person, marriage only enhances this relationship with God and is the supreme fulfillment. However, no matter how much a couple loves each other, they cannot communicate to God for one another because God dwells within each person. It is the fulfillment of *that* relationship, *that* marriage, which is the vertex of human development and human perfection. And it is this relationship with God that completes and perfects your relationship with your beloved.

Marriage is like all things—it is what you make of it. But if your foundation is divine love—that is love centered upon God, unselfish, unconditional love, compared to lustful, sensual love or selfish love—then you can achieve this ideal relationship.

Hello, Saint German. My name is Jana. My question to you is, as we come upon the new millennium there are many religious leaders throughout the world—American Indian tribal leaders and others—who believe something very dramatic is going to happen in the new millennium. I would like your impression of that. Thank you.

Things are *always* happening, aren't they? Whether you look at the calendar or not, whether you look at the year or not, something is always happening, isn't it? Earthquakes, floods and catastrophic event after catastrophic event take place.

If you were above the earth this moment you might observe this planet as being a potentially dangerous and tragic place. Why? Because at any one time, from outer space, you can see that there are thunder and lightening storms going on all over the earth. It is a proverbial light show! And there is snow falling some place and the wind is blowing elsewhere, and on and on. And this goes on all the time. These phenomena are of God's making. Without them, Mother Earth would not be served fully and correctly and man would suffer, as he does sometimes, from drought, crop failures, contaminated water supplies, and much more.

God's Timetable

As far as the idea of some cataclysmic event or some outstanding event due to a manmade date on the calendar, man will bring it on to himself if it happens. If there is enough momentum of fear, or anxiety behind your Y2K problem that we hear about in the world of spirit, then indeed, you will bring things upon yourselves.

The hoarding of food, of water, and so on creates an energy, a vibration. If enough people cooperate with such energy, that will cause it to build into a greater and greater force. There will be a backlash and there will come upon earth struggles that you have brought upon yourselves. Earthquakes take place resultantly from the "living" Mother Earth. Some of them are brought on by the gross and accumulated vibrations of man. Others are the natural result of Mother Earth needing to re-arrange her posture as internal changes are made. What is more, those who die in so-called cataclysmic events have met their end in that way by divine design. It was their way of taking their departure from the earth plane. Only when you come into the spirit world can you begin to fathom the overall reality of God's will.

So my "admonition," again using that word, is to think for yourself. Do not think that a God of love has created a world in which he should conform to manmade calendars and clocks. Rather, realize that when your time comes, it comes. If it is during a millennium beginning, then those who believe in such may say that it happened because it is the beginning of the millennium. But when the millennium begins, there will be many people who will not be touched at all: their wealth will not be touched, they will have plenty of food, they will experience no earthquakes, nor floods, nor storms. Their life will just continue. It is man's short-sighted view regarding all phenomena—spiritual and physical—that causes him to draw incomplete conclusions.

Does God work through symbolism? Yes. Does God work in tragedies? Of course. Does he cause them? No, he does not cause them. It is all by the evolution of things through divine law—things set in place from the beginning of time.

Susan: Saint Germain, it seems that time is passing more quickly than it used to and I seem to be having a harder time manifesting my needs, let alone my heart's desires. How do we do this? Is there a wrong way of asking? A right way of asking?

Harnessing Your Innate Power through Self-Mastery

It is case by case. As far as time is concerned, the older one gets, the closer you are to the possibility of transitioning to the spirit world. That means you are a gigantic step closer to God than those just starting out in life.

When you are closer to the sun, as some of the planets in this galaxy are, the sun rises and goes down more quickly than on earth. And so as you grow older, the seasons and the days pass faster because you are getting closer to that time when you are to make your transition and hopefully come more into the very presence of God. For all of you here who are 50 and above, you will experience this phenomenon if you already haven't experienced it. Am I not right? [**Yes.**]

As far as meeting your needs, we find in spirit that most of you have a wrong interpretation of God. And a wrong interpretation of what God is to do and what you are to do. Many of you struggle because of your incomplete ideas about yourself. The power that is within me and that I am able to harness through self-mastery, is available to all. I am not an exception.

Because of the way in which you were raised, most all of humanity does not know the strengths within, the power you all have to call upon. Most of you are in conscious and unconscious dilemmas because you have not yet learned to develop or exercise this innate divinity.

God wants to give you everything. He is not a stingy God. He does not ask for payment, as some ministers indicate that he does, in order to find salvation. Your ticket to God is love. That's all. Divine love! There is a spiritual reality, though. God can only come as close to you as you are close to him. While he dwells in you, he cannot prematurely manifest himself in you as he has in Jesus and other great masters until you are ready to receive him.

Some of you would be frightened if you were to see the great light that you are. You identify with your physical body, this very limited, limited thing. You do not identify with the light within. That light is so brilliant, so blinding, that it would overwhelm you to see it, for it is *the* very presence of God existing in you. And God is all light, the source of *all* light. Therefore, it is more brilliant than a million suns, for he also created the sun; light is because *he* is.

Now, why am I saying all this to you? Because you need to learn how to access this reality of yourself, your *higher* self. You need to let go of fear and insecurity, affirm and have ultimate and ultra conviction about God's presence in you. Then God can come very close. For those who have achieved complete oneness, there is manifested by God himself, food and clothing out of the air. There are those who dwell in caves in India who have spent their whole time loving God, and their needs are always met. Food appears. Their cave is warm without fire. They are protected from animals. And they know things without having to access the spirit world because God dwells in them and tells them innately and directly. The greatest need of all of you is the spiritual need to know your true self.

This is Helene. Saint Germain, thank you for being here. Would you mind expanding on free will and destiny?

What is the specific thing you want to know?

Some say that things are predestined and the major events in one's life cannot be changed—the people you encounter, major situations in your life, and the time of your death. Some people say that by free will you can change that. So I wanted to know your views on that. How much is destiny and how much is free will?

God's Spontaneity

Yes, I understand your question. First of all, God's love which you call "grace" when it descends and helps you or heals you— can supercede *all* physicality—ALL! That is why even a dead man can be made alive again. That's why people can see and hear again and why the many, many other miracles take place through God's miraculous healing grace.

God's love is what created you. You came out of the womb of God's love. You may think you came out of the womb of your mother. No, you came as a soul out of the womb of God. God is both male and female. God gave birth to you. As a soul, born of God, you are the same as God in the sense that you are made of the same elements with the same intelligence, with the same ability to love and be loved. Then you came to earth to take a physical body and were "created" in your mother. In your mother's womb you grew as a soul in the body waiting for your entrance on earth.

If God could create you out of love, then no matter what the situation in your life, he can also save you, out of love. He can intercede at any time. He does not always come personally. He may send some angelic force. He may send a spirit. Or he *may* come directly. Through his grace he may descend to you and lead you out of where you are, and allow his energy to manifest in order to make you whole or well. To answer your quest or question or fulfill your need.

Many miracles take place on earth every day that people think of as being coincidental or an accident. No. We are not indifferent to Mother Earth. Being connected to the source of all life, we are as earnest about Mother Earth's children as God is. So, too, we often manifest miracles, things that you do not see, do not know. How many times do you think that you might have been hit by a car but we intervened? How many times as a child do you think that you could have fallen from a high place and hurt yourself, or cut yourself, or done many things but were protected by us? So there are many miracles that you do not see. There is much intercessory work going on all the time—even tonight as we are sitting here—that you do not see.

Can life be prolonged, then? Yes. Yes. Yes. God's grace can descend and prolong life. Then we would have to say, "Life is in God's hands," wouldn't we? God is in charge.

How is it that certain individuals are able to see the past, present, and the future? It is because of their close proximity to God or God's descent into them and his ability to use their sensitivity. Some people have a longer antenna than others. That is, some people are more psychically open and sensitive and can pick up the radiation of God's presence, even without God manifesting specifically. God knows your past, present, and future, but allows you to feel the spontaneity of life by allowing you to think that there is free will.

It is not a game. You do the same thing with your children. You act as if you give them freedom. But in reality you keep them within the confines of what is safe and good for them. And so it is with God. The bird appears to be totally free as it flies hither and thither, but in reality if you were to track that bird, you would find it follows the same patterns all of its life within the confines of certain flight patterns and certain areas. So a bird looks spontaneous but is created to work instinctively, from the God-presence in it, within the confines of the territory assigned to it by God.

When you watch a whole flock of birds flying together—and all of you have seen this—and suddenly they all turn together, one direction and then the other and back and forth and back and forth, you wonder, how is it they do that?! Humans have come to call it instinct. We know it to be the very presence of God manifested holistically, creating this wonderful, wonderful artistic form moving spontaneously, suddenly in the sky. For God is seeing it all, is a part of it all, and God is enjoying it all. You think he created it just for you, but he created it for himself, too. And he enjoys all the various colors. He enjoys the roar of the river. He enjoys the fire of the volcano. He enjoys the bird on wing; the drop of rain on a blade of grass. He enjoys all things.

Your life, I can tell you without one moment's hesitation, regardless of the vicissitudes, is being held in the palm of the hand of God.

Linda: Thank you, Saint German, for explaining things so beautifully. I am very grateful to be here tonight. I was just wondering, as you explained the soul's birth from the womb of God, how that relates, then, to the idea of reincarnation?

Do you really want me to talk about that?

I was going to give you the option of not answering. [Laughter.]

The Virtuous Life

You are a great soul. I must say to you that while I tell you what I know—even though I am manifested in this body of Philip Burley—I am very choked up (even though my sentiment this moment seems out of context) because dear friends, I want you to understand how much God loves you.

You do not have to earn his love: just be! Just be yourself. And when you make mistakes due to ignorance or even overt mistakes knowingly, God does not throw down his anger and say, "That's it. I'm finished." How can God turn his back against himself? It's impossible. Many, many branches of religion have made God in *their* image. And they have attributed to the nature of God things that they, themselves, would never, ever do to their own children. Those who would say that God has created an everlasting hell for those who cannot accept or have not found him or his son or this person or that person, are only giving lip service to what they have learned. They are only parroting what they have heard.

But one day, either in this world or the next, their words will come back to them as being cruel, short-sighted and mean-spirited. Realizing that if they had been filled with divine love, then they would know there is no such a thing as a "lost" person; there is only ignorance and confusion.

I do not wish to speak about reincarnation. I only say this: (and my instrument seems to repeat what I say) whether there is reincarnation or a spirit return working with individuals from the spirit side, in either case it requires you to live a life that is virtuous and good. The outcome does not matter. You will know that soon enough. But what does matter is: if you do not live a life that is good, surely you will have to come back again in either case.

Saint Germain, this is Adrian. What was the purpose in our coming here, descending into this world where insanity seems to be so frequently the case?

Spend Time on the Inner Path

You each came here as a direct manifestation of the living God. It is this fundamental lack of knowledge regarding this reality about yourself that causes the craziness, the insanity. The message of who you are and what you are to do with your life is written inside of you. This is why the greatest teachers have said, "Know thyself."

You may look at the phenomena of the world and say there is insanity, but there is not a thing you can do about it. If each of you would stop looking at the world and look into yourself and resolve your *own* insanity, correct your own imperfections, and stay away from newspapers, gossip and negative talk, the world overnight would become heaven on earth. Do not stray from your own territory. Do not compare your path to another. Do not think that the grass is greener on the other side, but rather relish, appreciate, worship your own life and God within it.

Where is God? He is inside of you. How do you experience God? Through your very self. While angels and spiritual beings such as myself have appeared and given manifestations and done miracles and have been seen in our light body, our appearance is the lesser experience. The greater experience is to learn to go *inside*, to go beyond the layers of what you think is life, of what you think is true, and discover your own God-presence.

I spoke of that when I was on earth before. I speak of it again, because humanity has not yet learned. Sanity will return to each individual as each individual turns to God within. As long as you place God outside of yourself—someone to be reached in spatial time—you will be searching amiss. You will not find God, in the personal sense, except in yourself. When you truly entertain and approach your existence accordingly, your life will be turned around 180 degrees. It turns around completely because no longer do you make anyone else responsible for self. Nor do you blame the world. Nor are you searching for someone else to solve your problems. Nor are you seeking to find help outside of self.

How do you think we Masters achieved self mastery? It was not gained easily. It was not done overnight. Why do you think we teach, "Know thyself"? Why do you think we teach meditation? Why do you think we say over and over, "God is within."

Jesus *tried* to tell people. That was the greatest part of his message: "God is within." But you think of it in such abstract terms. You think of it in such distant ways. You do not think of it in the deepest personal way.

Go within. Spend time on the inner path. Ask and you shall receive. Seek to remove the blockages that your ignorance has placed before you. Seek to have the scales of half truths and falsehood removed from your eyes, and seek to experience God within. That experience transcends all experiences, even the marital experience, for it is all encompassing. It is 360° in every direction, on every plane. When you are in that state, there is no up, no down. There is no such a thing as "mine" and "yours." Everything is one. And you see not only the fact that you *came* from God, but you are an extension of God and therefore *are* God. You see all things are one!

Lisa: How can I best teach my children to achieve and maintain a good and progressively elevating spiritual life, as I do the same for myself, and yet have them live in the kind of world that we live in today?

Your Example of Unconditional Love

The answer to your question is very simple: see them as God. Do not compare them to you or you to them, or one to the other. See each one as unique and see them as your opportunity to love unconditionally.

Above all, if you cannot teach them of God directly, for whatever reason, then by all means, teach them by your example of unconditional love. Never condemn a child. Never tell them that they are this or that to the negative. Help them to understand themselves, but never, never condemn them.

It is monstrous what some parents say to their children, "You will never amount to anything." How terrible to say such a thing to a child! Some parents, in their own anger towards themselves slap their children without thought—hurting that soul—not just the face, not just the body, but that *soul!*

You are telling that child the total opposite of what they really are. They are divine, they are made of light. They are your privilege to serve and to love. When they need discipline, yes you need to discipline them. You need to give them boundaries. You need to give them direction, but never do it for any other reason than out of wisdom from divine love.

We all reap what we sow. And that is true with our children, as well. Rather, look upon your children as a gift, constantly! When there are difficulties and struggles ask yourself first—turn to self *first:* what is it that *I* am to learn from this experience? Go into the closet of yourself, or the literal closet, and meditate on this point. Contemplate before speaking. Many a war would never have taken place if people had taken just a few more days or weeks to think about the outcome, to allow the heat of the moment to cool down, to allow the irrationality of thought to pass by so the light within may have its way.

It takes a great amount of patience, love, and wisdom to raise a child from birth to adulthood. I know it is not easy, but you are the parent, and since you gave birth to them, you have the responsibility to act like a parent. To give to them from your storehouse of love.

If you are not centered upon goodness, if you are not centered upon God in the highest sense of experience, then how can you bring goodness to your children? You cannot. But as I said, at the very least give them unconditional love. Love them like yourself. Love them under all conditions, even when they disappoint you. Let them know you understand and have compassion and empathy. Put your arms around them, hold them tight. You may be, for them, their greatest hope. And it is that which will endear them to you. Not by catering to them. Not by giving into their immature whims, but by giving them truth with unconditional love.

We have come to the close of this hour. I know how much you appreciate the truth that we bring. But it is not because you don't already know the truth. If the truth was not already in you, you could not recognize it when it came from me. So all this information, all this knowledge, all this wisdom is waiting within you because *God* is in you and is the source of all this reality. Because we are celebrating in this season our beloved brother's birth, the master Jesus, then we should take seriously what he tried to do. He tried to teach the very things I am teaching you tonight and would, if he could have.

It's a different time, a different world. And whether you go to a new day on the calendar, a new year, a new millennium—whatever you call it—go to God. Stay with God. Especially, God within.

Thank you for being here. You can help the world most by applying what I have said to you in your individual life. Do not try to save the world. First, save yourself.

This is Saint Germain. My blessing is with you and abides with you at all times, as does the blessing of all the master teachers from above. Good night.   (VII)

Epilogue

Y APPEARANCE AT THE 2003 WESAK turned out to be a great turning point of my life. Dr. Joshua David Stone, founder of the annual Mount Shasta celebrations of the Wesak Festival, had told me that it would be and it was. In October and November of the same year I went to Japan to do spiritual readings and to give twelve seminars on varying topics. It was a great success to be followed by more. It was through a contact at the Wesak Festival that all of this happened.

I am exceedingly grateful to all the positive Forces of Heaven and Earth who opened the cosmic door into greater world service. I humbly seek to continue to follow the Golden Path. And with Saint Germain and other attendant spirit guides and teachers point the way to a better and higher life for all whom I meet in my own solemn but joyous spiritual walk on earth. Following is an edited copy of Saint Germain's and my talk at the Wesak Festival 2003.

Philip Burley and Saint Germain Speak

Wesak Festival, Mount Shasta, California
May 12, 2003

Philip Burley

OOD EVENING. THIS IS A LOVE FEAST, is it not? I'm so grateful to be here. It's been a long trek to come here. In the spring of 2002 I was about ready to end my career as a medium-channeler. I had wanted to do a greater work, to help more people. I was frustrated in not being able to do that even though I had been speaking to 70 to 80 thousand people per week on my radio show. I was also holding public meetings once a month in the Valley of the Sun and the turnout was less than I wanted it to be for all the effort that I put in with several of my staff.

I told God that *he needed to help me by opening the door of opportunity for greater and easier outreach and that I just would not continue unless he changed things for the better.* Saying this in a vein of utter frustration and impatience and in a rather loud voice, I simultaneously tore up a large stack of envelopes that were to go out with inserted invitations to my next local meeting in Scottsdale, Arizona. Having done this I felt a great release of frustration and was ready for a new adventure. Where? I was not sure. I just knew that I wanted an easier, faster, and broader way, than I had been experiencing, to help others find a spiritual life, God, and Spirit as I had. The very next day I received a call from Dr. Stone's office telling me that he wanted to know if I would be a speaker in May of 2003 at the Wesak Festival at Mount Shasta, California.

I was deeply moved at both the invitation and the synchronicity of the call. I knew that someone "upstairs" had been working overtime to make all of this happen. I knew that person to be Saint Germain! And this is how I got here!

Prior to my channeling Saint Germain, I have a few things I want to share with you to give you a little knowledge, or a little experience with me, and the dimension at which I work with Spirit. You know in this kind of work you spend a lot of time alone. You have to if you are going to be good and authentic. And that time is spent in prayer and meditation—in quiet times of waiting on and experiencing Spirit.

Prior to 9-11, I had a visitation from an angel. This has happened to me periodically throughout my life. In fact, at the advent of my work as a medium-channeler, an angel came to me in a vision-dream saying that he was sent by the Father to announce my mission and to guide me in that mission. That is another story.

In the visitation of the angel prior to 9-11, the angel said, "I come to you from the Father. And I want to show you America." As he intoned these words I found that we were standing on the eastern shore of the United States and he was a giant and so was I (both over a mile high) as we peered down on New York City below. The angel pointed to the north to Boston, and said, "That

213

is the center of your intellectual prowess. And you take great pride as a nation in your educational institutions and your intellect."

Then he pointed to the south, to Washington, D.C. And said, "Here is your political center, in which you take pride in your political power and prowess around the world as a nation." There was no condemnation, no judgment; just the making of a comment.

And then he pointed down to New York City. And he said, "And this is a city which is your financial power center in which you take pride as the core of the wealth of your nation." And as I looked down, I could see the head of a giant. He was lying on his left side, and I saw that he had bright red hair. The angel said, "The red hair,"—so red; it was an unnatural red—"represents lust for money, lust for power; the misuse of sexual energy." New York City lay under his head and served as his pillow. From this point his body stretched out across our nation, all the way to the west coast where his feet were resting in Los Angeles. He was a sleeping giant!

Remaining at my side the angel continued, "Come with me, I want to take you to the west coast." So we walked down the eastern shore of the Atlantic to Florida in giant strides. We then, also in giant steps, crossed Florida and the Gulf of Mexico. As we did so we could look up and see the United States. From this vantage point—mid the Gulf—it was easy see the giant stretched out across America. I took particular notice that he was covered with a quilt whose patches were each state cut out and sown together.

Quickly we reached the west coast and walked north to the area of Los Angeles. The angel and I, at this point, stood on the shores of the Pacific Ocean with L.A. just in the distance.

The angel gestured for me to follow him ashore saying, "Come, I must show you." We were standing near the quilt-covered feet of the sleeping giant when the angel reached down and pulled up the quilt for me to see what was going on under the cover. To my shock, dismay, and disgust I saw two huge, huge rats, at least fifteen to twenty feet tall, standing on their back feet chewing on the feet of the sleeping giant! No words can adequately convey this scene and the emotion of it all.

Why do I tell you this story? First, it is a true story; I did not make it up. Secondly, when God sends an angel to convey such a message it is to be taken seriously. And of course the meaning of the dream became vividly clear after the tragedy of 9-11. This dream was given because our nation has been a sleeping giant. And the day after 9-11 I went on the radio and shared this dream with my listeners and since then the dream has gone around the world on the Internet.

The *unenlightened* are the sleeping giant. They need the light; they need to be enlightened. Brothers and sisters, you are their hope, you have the light. Whether you ever *speak* the light, *be* the light. Speak and live the truth! The successful future of our nation lies in the hands of those people who know they have the light and know how to make it shine, to awaken and enlighten the sleeping giant. I admire you all so much for being here; just being here to be even a little light shining out into the darkened world to bring illumination... enlightenment.

Prior to this Wesak event, I had been praying urgently to God, to our Father in heaven, and asking him to show me my *eternal self.* I'd really been praying and praying. And about two months ago, Saint Germain woke me up one morning seemingly in response to my prayer request. It was as if I was wide awake and in my spirit as he literally took me out of my body. You know, my spirit-self just rose up and went with him as he took me about ten feet away from the bed. In a most loving but commanding way he pointed at my body, and said, "Now, watch!"

Suddenly, there was this brilliant flash of blue light and my whole body lit up inside. It was totally illuminated. Without missing a beat he said, "That is your eternal being, and it shall never, never die, It will never go away." And then that energy coursed throughout my body, going to every atom, every cell of my body, illuminating every part of me, and he said, "That, too, shall never go away."

Why I love Saint Germain so much is because he is about individual human freedom. I don't know what he's going to talk about tonight; I never know what he's going to say, and I don't know what he said unless I listen to the tape. I feel so grateful to be here at Mount Shasta with him.

I'm going to have them play some music, and then I'm going to take a seat as they play it. And I would like to have you stand. I know first of all, you do get tired sitting, but also, this song is entitled "Holy Ground" and implies that we are standing on holy ground, which we are, because God is here with us. And while the song plays—Germain usually allows it to play to the end—then he comes through. Again, I don't know what he's going to do, if he's going to allow for questions and answers or if he's going to give a talk?

After he transfigures over me, some of you may see the violet light, as some audience members have at other meetings. And still, others of you may see his face appear over mine as others have testified in the past too. All of you will hear a change in the vocalization. Also, sometimes it takes him a little while to get into my energy, because there's an adjustment or lowering of his vibration to get into my frequency of thought and emotion. So I'll do my best, and so will he. But I again thank you for this blessing of being here before you and to have this opportunity to share beloved Saint Germain. God bless you. May we have the music?

Saint Germain

[Chuckles loudly as he first comes through Philip.] I am here. This is Saint Germain, please be seated.

 come with many of those beings whose names you mentioned today, whom you called out. They are here to echo your call, to call you. It is a great, great joy for me to come here again, after 73 years of my original appearance on this august mountainside. I came here because of the same reasons that you come here. It is a place of holiness. It is a place where you can remove yourself from the world and be with God.

I would like to begin with a prayer of gratitude and thanksgiving to the Creator, our Father and Mother:

Almighty God,

We are here gathered in your presence, that you have given us the blessing of coming together for the great purpose of the liberation of ourselves and of mankind. You have brought us here to learn from each other, and to take home with us a greater light, through greater awareness of ourselves and of each other.

Father, your love, as manifested here today, and the coming days, is so sweet—so almighty, so all-embracing of each one. May each one feel your presence in a way that they have never felt it before. May your love, may your power reverberate all the way down to the bottom of their feet. Throughout every atom of their being, may they feel the vibration, the mighty power, yet personal reality of your love. That which you have given to me, Father, I have sought to give to others.

Thank you for this blessing of allowing me to use this instrument, and to come to the earth plane in this way, at this time. And to be here for this Wesak Festival. May you be glorified. May you have your dream in each one of us and collectively come to pass. All of this I pray in the mighty names of all of the great masters and teachers and in the name of each individual here, I ask this prayer.

Amen.

Some people have asked me, would I like to reincarnate? Someone approached my medium prior to my coming up here, saying that there is someone here, up on Mount Shasta, who looks like me. Why should I want to come back, when I have an instrument like this to work through? In this way, I can be between two worlds and that is the purpose.

You see, I am able to be here with you, but at the same time, as a master who has learned how to manipulate the energies of my being and of the universe, I can be in other places at the same time. Whereas, if I'm embodied I do not have this same freedom. Of course, it may be easier to take a body on

218

earth through the womb of a woman and be born again, but being spirit, I have the privilege of walking on the edge between two worlds, and bringing forth what the Father wants me to bring unhindered by a physical body.

I do want you to know that my greatest purpose in being here is for your liberation through understanding. Through understanding who you are, why you came to this earth plane, and what it is that you are to achieve in this lifetime, through this body.

There are many here [in the spirit world] who have not yet reached the higher plateaus as you have in your spiritual attainment. They are greatly envious of you knowing what you know and they wish they were embodied also so that they might derive the benefit that comes from the mutual exchange of energy flowing between your spirit and your body, centered upon the higher truths that you know and live.

So while you are in this body, while you are a spirit residing in this body, take nothing for granted. Every breath is one less breath that you will take on this earth. Every meal that you eat is one less meal that you will eat. And all for one purpose did you come into this earth plane, and that is to realize the fullness of self.

I am famous, as you know, for the **I AM** teachings. Some have been misinterpreted in some ways, but for the most part, people got what I was saying. What I learned in my going up the mountain of life—that's why I love this mountain, Mount Shasta, it is a great symbol for attainment... And I started to say, as you look at its peak, it looks challenging to climb. And it is! But yet it is necessary. It is necessary to live this life out seeking to overcome all the obstacles that would stand in your way, and would keep you from realizing your own God presence.

I revealed to this man, Philip Burley, his inner spark, the inner divine essence in reality, because he asked me to. And being faithful to the call in my using of him, he gained the merit by which I could do that. Such so called miracles are available to all people. You have but to so seek and so desire them. What he did not tell you was how it transformed his life. How he saw himself differently, my dear, dear friends. How he saw himself as an eternal, divine being made of eternal, ever-glowing, ever-growing light!

It's one thing to say we are eternal. It is one thing to write about being eternal, as earlier, on this same stage this lovely Virginia Essene spoke and I stood by listening, she spoke about the necessity of becoming that higher self. Those are not her words, but that is what she meant. To not only read such words, but to become those words, to be divine, to become a holy person, to become all that you can become in God!

God came to earth in you. Each of you is nothing less than the radiation of God's presence on earth. That is what I meant by the great **I AM**. God projected from his holy heart, with all the zeal of a child in exploring life and creating life, with all the love and passion and compassion of a parent waiting for the birth of a child, he did deposit you here on earth in this physical form. He thought of you for eons of time before he ever manifested you, before you ever took birth in this body.

And what came with you? The full map. All the instructions came with you. What is your job? To find them. To open up the box of self and find the instructions inside. That is the major part of his plan for you on this earth plane. This life is therefore about discovering self through understanding the principles by which to reveal self. Do I make myself clear? [**Yes.**]

And you know, dear friends, there are many things I wanted to say when I was on the earth plane, and I could not. It was not time. And the particular instrument I used then was limited as all instruments are limited. That's why there are many of you. Because God must speak through many channels. And then we braid together the truth out of the collection of things we read and we study from many sources. That's why the more of the right spiritual education you can get, the more you can know yourself, and the more you can know God.

So God invested himself in you, and he knows you personally. People call me a being of great love. Was I always that way? That's my secret! But, I discovered God within me. I discovered first, in my meditations, when I was quite young, I discovered first that God loved me. Isn't that a great revelation? To know by direct experience, by the emanation of God's love to you, and through you, that you are loved is the most valuable and wonderful thing in life. In that kind of love, there is such promise and freedom.

In that kind of love, you can forgive yourself of all things, for God's love is unconditional, that I can tell you. If you go from here, after these few days together, and you learn only that, that God loves you under all conditions, ALL conditions, then you have a gained a great step forward upon the mountain of life.

But more than that, because God knows you personally, intimately, he can tell you, as Jesus said, the number of hairs on your head. He could even tell you the number of atoms of which you are made. In reality, he is the breath of your breath.

He is the heartbeat of your heartbeat. When you look out at all the beauty of nature, he celebrates and feels it through you, how he is connected to you. You are constantly in the circuit of God's eternal love. And you can never be taken out. And that love courses through you from the beginning of time to the end of time. In other words, forever, and forever, and forever and forever shall you exist.

Tonight, God is here. Where? Everywhere. There's not one atom in this room that does not contain the energy of God, the love of God, the presence of God.

Jesus and I have discussed many times his frustration in trying to get people to understand that God lives in them. They could not comprehend what Jesus was saying when they were used to seeing God in a statue outside of them.

God lives in you. Otherwise, you could not live. Today, it has been said many times, not only by Saint Germain but by many wise individuals. If God would cease to be this moment, so would you. You are living in the life stream of God's love, God's thought, God's presence. Do you feel that? How can you increase that?

I'm telling you nothing new. I'm repeating to you what you already know to be true, because you came in with all this information in the encyclopedia of self. It's a part of the instructions. So you can, as it were, find yourself by finding God within.

I must go. Again, it is my great, great joy to have been here tonight. To have delivered a few words of encouragement to you, and to have been able to use this instrument to do so has given me great, great happiness. Feel free to call on me at any time. I am yours at your beck and call. I may not have all of the answers, but I have a lot of them.

What I revealed to Mr. Ballard here on the side of this mountain is only a tiny dew drop of information compared to the tomes of information available. You don't need to know it all. You only need to know yourself, and then you can dip into those larger volumes of information and find your way further and further along.

The secret to life is not hidden. The secret to attaining spiritual perfection is not hidden. It's right within your Self. Therefore, be loyal to your script. Do not compare your life to the life of another, for the grass is not—is not—is not—is not greener on the other side. Be happy with you, and each time you look in the mirror, if you must in order to fall in love with self, kiss the mirror. Kiss it until you're so much in love with self, you can't see anything else. Because until you do that, dear friends, in the healthy sense of the word, you cannot unfold the mighty **I AM** presence within you, God within you.

Have I captured your attention? Do you appreciate my appearance here? I do not say this in order to "bait" you to use your earthly word. But because I want you to hear *your* earnest desires that you may be inspired to be all that you can be. That you can be a beacon of light as Saint Germain is, and all these other saints and all the other master teachers, that you can shine for your nation and the world.

You are light individuals scattered around the world. Let your light shine. Tell others about this festival. Expand it if you can, to bring greater and greater numbers. And remember the power that you have to release. Even as I showed this medium his power; it resides in all of you, and plentifully.

And if you ask me, I may come to your bedside, too. And I may take you out of your body. And I may show you your explosive self. A light that shall never ever, ever go out. That Self will shine forever and ever, blending with, melting into, becoming totally one with, your eternal, ever-expanding God Presence.

Now I'm going to take my leave. And if I've left you a few minutes extra, use them to celebrate yourselves and the God presence within you in the closing ceremony to this evening.

And as you drift off to sleep tonight, call us all in. We'll come. We'll surround you. We'll lift you up. We may even take you out of your body. In fact, let's all meet tonight on cloud 9. [Laughter.]

Or better yet, let's meet on top of Mount Shasta! [Laughter and applause.]

Our love follows you wherever you go. This is Saint Germain, beloved ones. God bless you.

References: Preface and Discourses

PREFACE – PART II

> *The Life and Times of Saint Germain*
> **The Inner View – Adventures in Spirit**
> May 9, 2001, Show #111

DISCOURSE ONE: SCALING THE SUMMIT –
MOUNT SHASTA WESAK FESTIVAL

> Circle of the Eternal Flame
> January 20, 2003, Phoenix, Arizona
> To Staff of Mount Shasta, Wesak Festival
> *Copyright 2003 by Philip Burley - All Rights Reserved*

DISCOURSE TWO: TRUE ENLIGHTENMENT

> Circle of the Eternal Flame
> February 17, 2003, Phoenix, Arizona
> To Staff of Mount Shasta, Wesak Festival
> *Copyright 2003 by Philip K. Burley - All Rights Reserved*

DISCOURSE THREE: THE HALLMARK OF YOUR LIFE

> Spiritual Reading – Philip Burley, Medium
> CR-046-96F
> July 30, 1996, Phoenix, Arizona
> *Copyright 1996 by Philip K. Burley - All Rights Reserved*

DISCOURSE FOUR: MULTI-FACETED YOU

> Circle of the Eternal Flame
> February 3, 2003, Phoenix, Arizona
> To Staff of Mount Shasta, Wesak Festival
> *Copyright 2003 by Philip K. Burley - All Rights Reserved*

DISCOURSE FIVE: **LOVE IS THE REIGNING PRINCIPLE**
Circle of the Eternal Flame
Special Meeting, – March 30, 2003 Morning Session
To Staff of Mount Shasta, Wesak Festival, Phoenix, Arizona
Copyright 2003 by Philip K. Burley - All Rights Reserved

DISCOURSE SIX: **EVER FOLLOW THE GUIDING STAR**
Spiritual Reading, Philip Burley, Medium
CR-049-96F
August 5, 1996, Phoenix, AZ
Copyright 1996 by Philip K. Burley - All Rights Reserved

DISCOURSE SEVEN: **GOD'S GAME OF LIFE**
Circle of the Eternal Flame
Special Meeting – March 30, 2003 Afternoon Session
To Staff of Mount Shasta, Wesak Festival, Phoenix, Arizona
Copyright 2003 by Philip K. Burley - All Rights Reserved

DISCOURSE EIGHT: **THE MAGNIFICENT REALITY OF SELF**
Spiritual Reading, Philip Burley, Medium
To an Individual (Female) in a Personal Reading
July 24, 1996, Phoenix, AZ
Copyright 1996 by Philip K. Burley - All Rights Reserved

DISCOURSE NINE: **WEAVING GOD'S TAPESTRY**
Saint Germain Speaks – October 10, 1996
Seattle, Washington
Copyright 1996 by Philip K. Burley - All Rights Reserved

DISCOURSE TEN: **LIFE IS ETERNAL, CYCLIC, & GROWING**
The Inner View – Adventures in Spirit
January 3, 2001, Show #KF93
Copyright 2001 by Philip K. Burley - All Rights Reserved

References: Questions & Answers With Saint Germain

The reader will note ( ) with a roman numeral after a set of questions. The following are the references for the time and place of those sessions.

I   Saint Germain Speaks to the Circle of the Eternal Flame
       February 17, 2003, Phoenix, Arizona
       To Staff of Mount Shasta, Wesak Festival
          Copyright 2003 by Philip K. Burley - All Rights Reserved

II   Saint Germain Speaks to the Circle of the Eternal Flame
       Special Meeting – March 30, 2003 (morning session)
       To Staff of Mount Shasta, Wesak Festival, Phoenix, Arizona
          Copyright 2003 by Philip K. Burley - All Rights Reserved

III   Saint Germain Speaks to the Circle of the Eternal Flame
       Special Meeting – March 30, 2003 (afternoon session)
       To Staff of Mount Shasta, Wesak Festival – Phoenix, Arizona
          Copyright 2003 by Philip K. Burley - All Rights Reserved

IV   Spiritual Reading (CR-040-96M) Philip Burley, Medium
       July 22, 1996, Phoenix, Arizona
          Copyright 1996 by Philip K. Burley - All Rights Reserved

V   Saint Germain Speaks – October 10, 1996 , Seattle, Washington
          Copyright 1996 by Philip K. Burley - All Rights Reserved

VI Spiritual Reading (CR-050-96F) Philip Burley, Medium
    August 6, 1996, Phoenix, Arizona
        Copyright 1996 by Philip K. Burley - All Rights Reserved

VII Saint Germain Speaks. Christmas AIM Meeting
     December 13, 1999, Scottsdale, Arizona
         Copyright 1999 by Philip K. Burley - All Rights Reserved

Historical Information on Saint Germain

The Count of Saint-Germain, by Isabel Cooper-Oakley, Rudolph Steiner Publications, Blauvelt, New York, 1970

The Most Holy Trinosophia, of the Comte de St.-Germain, Introduction and Commentary by Manly P. Hall, The Philosophical Research Society, Inc., Los Angeles, CA, 1983

Phoenix, Arizona

For general inquiries send an email to
PB@PhilipBurley.com, or write to:

Adventures in Mastery, LLC (AIM)
P.O. Box 43548
Phoenix, AZ 85080

For more information about Philip Burley
and the work of
Adventures in Mastery, LLC,
please visit this website:
www.PhilipBurley.com

CPSIA information can be obtained
at www.ICGtesting.com
Printed in the USA
LVHW040815220719
624829LV00001B/61